W9-APG-339

Go Ahead ASK ANYTHING

Go Ahead ASK ANYTHING

ANSWERS TO YOUR QUESTIONS ABOUT LIFE

JIM LYON

Stylos Records
Anderson, Indiana

GO AHEAD. ASK ANYTHING.

This book is printed on acid-free, elemental chlorine-free paper.

Stylos Records
P.O. Box 6
Anderson, Indiana 46064
Published 2011

ISBN 978-0-9834002-1-9

Project Management and Editing by Andrew Lyon
Book Design by J. Kevin Majeski | JKevinCreative.com
Production Assistance: Jenny Fultz | FultzDesign.com
Editing by Barbara Dick
Creative Direction and Development Management by Stylos Records & Entertainment

MANUFACTURED IN THE UNITED STATES OF AMERICA
11 12 13 14 15 16 17 18 19 20—10 9 8 7 6 5 4 3 2 1

"Jim Lyon is the most brilliant mind I know preaching today. Now he shares his insights in this book. It doesn't just answer questions, it knocks down walls and opens doors to new insights into God, you and the tough parts of life. You will not be disappointed."

Steve Arterburn
Founder of New Life Ministries, Women of Faith,
Author of *Every Man's Battle*

I've had the privilege of hearing Jim Lyon teach and speak for many years. I have learned that there are no questions that scare him. He always strives to answer questions in a way that is thoughtful, biblically grounded and truth-giving. He tackles the tough life questions with frank honesty and deep compassion; always offering grace. I am grateful to call him my pastor. I am blessed to call him my friend.

Sandi Patty
Christian Recording Artist and Author

Jim Lyon is a man who dares to plunge into the depths of God's heart in search of answers. His poetic rhythms, adventuresome lifestyle, and daring questions add dimension to everything he writes. This book is an invitation to throw open your doubts and embrace God's willingness to meet us where we are...in our wonderings and our wandering.

Patsy Clairmont
Women of Faith Speaker
Author of *Kaleidoscope*

Contents

Introduction 1

Question 10: Illegal Immigration 11

Question 9: God: The Decider? 29

Question 8: Sex, Church and Straight Talk 43

Question 7: Death and What's Next 63

Question 6: Choice and Destiny: Free Will and Predestination 81

Question 5: The Voice of God 95

Question 4: The Irreversible Gift? 111

Question 3: Christianity Compared 127

Question 2: Applying Scripture 141

Question 1: Homosexuality 157

Epilogue 175

References 179

Introduction

It's a big world out there. Diverse, too. Sometimes we are confined by—limited by—the small worlds in which we live. The familiar. The predictable. The manageable. The world that has already been experienced by us.

Every now and then, we bump into people who come from different worlds. Their language, customs, culture, cuisine, and challenges may be worlds apart from our own. But, in the end, doesn't everyone fundamentally face the same questions about life? Is it possible that while our contexts may frame the questions in a variety of ways, we all still wonder about the same things?

When I was 19, I had the chance to travel abroad for the first time. Growing up as an only child, I had two cousins, John and Tim Worthen,[1] who were like brothers to me—and they invited me to explore Europe with them one summer. We landed in London, obtained access to a new Volkswagen, and spent the next six weeks camping in Britain and on the continent. From London to Venice to Geneva to Brussels to Rome, we dove into a world half-a-globe away from our own in Seattle. I spent my 20th birthday in Paris. And, at the last, we spent a week attending the 1972 Olympic Games in Munich. The 1972 Games are these days remembered principally for the terror attack on the Israeli Olympic Team, and that awful tragedy has, in our collective memory, trumped the athletic triumphs of record-breaking athletes like the American swimmer, Mark Spitz. My experience in Europe *per se*—and at the Munich Games in particular—raised deep and important questions for me: about life, about God, about the paths I would choose, and about the contradictory world and events that moved in all directions around me. I found myself staring down questions I had never before thought to ask and, at times, had been afraid to ask.

Where was God in the Munich murders? Where was God in the jagged edges of the modern conflict in what the ancient Romans called Palestine and the Old Testament named Israel? Where was God in the stylized ritual of Catholic veneration of the "holy steps" at the Cathedral of St. John Lateran in Rome? And where was God in the 19th century legacy of the American Protestant tradition in which I had been raised? Where was God, anyway? Is there a God? And, why did I have to follow the conservative rules of conduct with which I had been clothed since childhood and which, before I celebrated my 20th birthday in Paris, seemed so obviously tailored for me? Why was I so defined by rules grounded in the Christian Bible? And why was that book so "all that," anyway? Were there any rules that really existed apart from human convention? Why can't I just be like everybody else, acting out like other 20-year old guys?

Once I allowed myself to ask them, the questions tumbled out of my heart and head fast and furiously, and by the time I boarded my flight from London's Heathrow for the long flight over the pole back home to Seattle, I wasn't sure of anything.

Questions can be frightening. They can lead us to walk onto uncertain terrain; they can leave us longing for the world we left behind. The familiar. The predictable. The manageable. The world already experienced, before the questions.

One of the most vivid memories of my days in Munich during the Olympic Games was formed, not in one of the dramatic competition venues or by the dark headlines from the terror attack, but instead during a sunny afternoon in the Marienplatz. The Marienplatz is the iconic center of postcard Munich, a vast public square in the city's center, in the summertime ablaze with flowers, boxed by classic Bavarian architecture and a towering clock tower, complete with *glockenspiel*. One day, before the Palestinian invasion of the Israeli team's housing, I walked through the square and found people from all over the world seated on the benches and under café umbrellas. They wore every kind of dress imaginable and spoke, it seemed, more languages than Babel. At every glance, I could see gestured conversations, animated and engaged: people from all across the planet talking, listening, sharing.

As I watched more closely, I noticed that on every bench, at every café table, the same conversation appeared to be taking place. This global crowd all seemed to be cementing relationships with pictures of their families. Photographs were studied, pulled out of wallets, retrieved from purses. And although I was not fluent in any language but English, the message everywhere was unmistakable: "This is my sister," or "These are my parents," or "This is my home," and "Do you have a picture of the most important relationships in your life?" The irreducible prime of all human relationships, the common thread of all people everywhere: I want to be known. In the end, no matter what the context of my culture or ideas, I long to be valued, respected, understood. Furthermore, I want to understand, to make sense of the world around me, to know those who share it with me. This hunger cannot be satisfied apart from our relationships.

In that moment, my world was both expanded to circumnavigate the globe and telescoped to focus on my own little place in it. I, too, had pictures of my mom and dad, my house at the end of the dead-end street, in a wooded ravine, in north Seattle. I had dreams I wanted to share, also, nourished by the experiences of my childhood. Deep down inside I realized that my world wasn't really all that different from everyone else's. If my need to be known and understood was really not all that different from that of others, perhaps my questions were not all that different either. Surely everybody, if they are nakedly honest would admit that they've harbored tough questions, too—questions that might challenge the norms of their community or beg for answers beyond the conventional. Maybe our worlds are not small because we prefer the familiar and predictable but because we're afraid to ask questions. We're afraid to ask anything and everything. We're certainly afraid to ask at church.

Eventually, after my once-in-a-lifetime European vacation, I returned to my undergraduate work at the University of Washington and began to sort things out. I stared down the questions, grappled with different sets of answers, made some choices, and, over time, proved their worth true. I also learned that there would be more tough questions as life unfolded, that I could not be healthy if I attempted to avoid or suppress them, that I should not be afraid of them, that everybody (including me) longs for answers to help make sense of this confused world, and that pursuing answers through the lens of an objective truth, beyond myself, has real merit.

Fast-forward 36 years. I am traveling again, this time in remote, northeast India. My cousin, John, still like a brother to me, is with me again, as we explore radio production opportunities for the English broadcast that I host in North America, *ViewPoint.* John has come along as a grip, helping carry the production equipment and facilitate taping interviews. Shillong is nestled high above the humid lowlands of Indian Bengal and Islamic Bangladesh. A city of nearly one million, it hugs steep, forested hillsides, with a temperate climate that reminds me of San Francisco without the fog. It is the capital of the Indian state of Megahalya, sandwiched in a geographically strategic intersection of south Asian people groups and nations (including China, Myanmar, Bangladesh, Sikkim, and more). It has an air of Shangri La about it, bearing the marks of the fictional and mysterious Eden-like city lost in time in the novel *Lost Horizons.*

As John and I drank from the exotic well of this out-of-this-world stop on the way to who knew what else, hosted by some of the most brilliant and sage Indian Christians I have ever met (and I've met many in nearly 30 years of visits to the subcontinent), we marveled, once more, at the way in which people are the same everywhere. We ask the same questions, have the same hopes, face the same fears as everyone else. Yes, a city steeped in India's Hindu traditions is, on many levels, very different from the English-Scandinavian-American frontier city of Seattle from which we both came. Ultimately, though the languages, curried chicken, and theological garb are different, we all have questions, and we are all sometimes afraid of them.

John mentioned to me that his pastor, Mark Driscoll at the Mars Hill Church in Seattle, was walking through a preaching series in which he had invited the congregation to ask questions. A website had been developed at Mars Hill that could receive questions and line them up in a way that people could then vote on them. Which questions would you like to have answered at Mars Hill, if you could choose five or ten, etc.?[2]

Driscoll, of course, is famed for his daring in the pulpit and for his straightforward delivery. He commands the stage (and I don't just mean the stage of his local church, but a larger, worldwide audience) with definition and boldness. He is not afraid of the questions or afraid to give answers.

My interest was piqued by John's report from Mars Hill, as we found ourselves winding down a treacherous, cliff-hanging, impossibly twisting mountain road from Shangri La to the dusty plains of Guwahati. I wondered if I might attempt such a series in my own world, opening the doors for questions in the American heartland, since I now live and preach in central Indiana, near Indianapolis, at a church called Madison Park.

On the way home from India, John and I (and two other members of our *ViewPoint* team, Scott and Mike) stopped over in Amsterdam. Many flight connections between India and the States meet there. I have been to Amsterdam many times and found it fascinating. Like Paris, Amsterdam escaped destruction during the Second World War. Its centuries-old architecture, picturesque canals, and stunning art collections (think Rembrandt, Van Gogh, Vermeer) make it worth the trip. It was the home of Anne Frank, and the closeted attic in which she wrote her famous diary before being apprehended by the Nazi occupation is one of the most inspiring—and sobering—places I have ever been.

In the days of the Reformation, Amsterdam was a powerhouse of transformational change within Christendom. The principle of *sola Scriptura* (Scriptures alone) and devotion to a holy God, revealed in the Gospel of Jesus, thundered from its pulpits. Dutch missionaries went far and wide from its docks, following in the footsteps of Holland's merchant class, carrying the same message. And yet today, few people imagine Amsterdam as a buckle in the European Bible belt (if such a belt can even be imagined these days). How and why did Amsterdam move from its pedestal of biblical energy to today's emblematic address for everything but? Speak the word Amsterdam anywhere in the world in the 21st century and images of prostitutes beckoning from street windows and legalized drugs overwhelm history's church steeples and Bible readings. Why? And why not? There I go, asking questions again. Just like when I first visited Europe.

Weeks before arriving in Amsterdam, I had attempted to set up interviews with a variety of sources, seeking to build a *ViewPoint* radio program around this question. Perhaps, there would be something to learn and offer to other communities facing the future if we explored Amsterdam's road to the present. I contacted businesses, churches, museums and more, seeking a diverse collection of voices.

One place I also contacted was the Prostitute Information Center. When I sent an e-mail to the Center, I understood it to be a research center that academics and sociologists accessed to understand the sex trade, for which Amsterdam is so well known. It is that, in a way, but I would soon discover it was also much more.

By the time I arrived in Amsterdam, with my *ViewPoint* team in tow, only one of my contacts for interviews had come through. None of the businesses, churches, or arts centers were interested in being interviewed. Some did not reply at all. The only positive response came from, yes, you guessed it, the Prostitute Information Center.

I wondered if I should go through with the interview. It was only one voice, after all, and I wasn't sure I could build a program around a single perspective. But the Center had issued an invitation and offered an appointment. My traveling companions all agreed that it would be better to show up than to stand the Center up. We checked the address and looked for the office, in the heart of Amsterdam's most historic—and most provocative—red light district. And there it was: a storefront, facing the Olde Kirk, one of Amsterdam's most historic and elegant houses of worship. The Center was also in a line of storefront-prostitution glass doors, in which women gesture to every man passing by to stop in and do some business. All four of us stared at the ground as we approached the Center's door. Every man in Amsterdam learns quickly that if you make eye contact with the women in the windows, the lock can begin to draw even the most reluctant to the doorstep (especially if you've been in the outback of the subcontinent for several weeks alone with three other guys).

When we entered the Center, a woman I gauged to be in her late 20s or early 30s greeted us. I introduced myself and asked for the Center's founder who had agreed to the interview. The woman behind the counter explained that the founder had been unexpectedly called out of town, that the Center offered its regrets, but that an interview was still possible if I was open to talking with this woman at the counter. Her name was Anya. She was well acquainted with the Center's work, history, and storyline.

John unpacked the equipment, and the microphones were set in place. I began to ask Anya a few set-up questions for the broadcast and soon discovered that not only does the Center facilitate sociological research, it is, first of all, a kind of "better business bureau" for Amsterdam's sex trade. It helps potential customers understand how to negotiate with the sex workers (as they are described), what prices are reasonable for what sex acts, and it advocates for those involved.

Whoops. This wasn't exactly the interview I had in mind. Then Anya disclosed, quite matter-of-factly, that she was a prostitute and found the job much more rewarding and satisfying than her previous career as a second grade teacher in Toronto.

What? My mind was flooded with questions. No, I shouldn't ask them. I hesitated. Then, I decided to go ahead and ask some—on tape, for *ViewPoint*: a weekly radio program owned by Christians Broadcasting Hope.

Aren't you afraid? ("No.") Don't you ever feel vulnerable? ("No. Now facing that classroom—and the parents—when I taught public school in Toronto, that made me feel vulnerable.") Aren't there health risks involved? ("No. We're all checked thoroughly by doctors every month; I always make men wear condoms. No problem.") What do you think of the men who hire you? Do you respect them? ("It's like any job; if I sold insurance, I'd have some clients I liked and some I didn't like; it's like that as a sex worker, too.") Don't you feel bad for the wives who may be left behind when you have sex with someone else's husband for money?" ("No. It's not my business where they come from or who they leave behind. These men make their own choices; they have to own them.") Why do you think men come here? ("So they can be free to be who they want to be; when they're here with women like me, they don't have to pretend; they ask for what they want, and they get what they want. It's honest and that simple. Everywhere else they're afraid to be who they want to be.")

We talked some more, and I asked if she had a private life, a boyfriend, a husband, etc. ("Yes, thank you, a boyfriend; he's not bothered by what I do and actually finds it interesting"). I pointed to the magnificent church building across the cobblestoned square, its steeple piercing the grey and moody sky. How do you square what you do with the shadow of that church and what it represents in Dutch history? What do you think about the values—and the God—it represents?

She looked at me and replied, "When I was a little girl, I went to church some. But I gave it up as a child; I haven't been for many years. The church—that church—no church—ever has spoken to me. It's irrelevant. It doesn't speak to me; it doesn't give me the time of day; I don't give it the time of day."

Pause. I glanced at John, Scott, and Mike. There it was. The answer to my original question, implausibly unearthed at the Prostitute Information Center. How did Amsterdam change over the years from one of the world's most influential centers of Gospel life to a poster child for sexual license? The church stopped speaking to people like Anya.

I then explained to Anya who I was and how much I appreciated her honest and authentic answers to my questions. I also explained that I had made a promise to my wife when I married her that I would reserve my body for her and her alone as long as our lives shall last and that, as a Christian man, I was bound by that promise and glad to be. We were just a few weeks away from Christmas, and I told her we would pray that the Lord would bless and encourage her this Christmas, and disclose Himself to her in wonderful, life-giving ways. She seemed quite surprised, was very gracious, and thanked us for coming.

When we walked outside into the late afternoon twilight, another woman, Stella, approached us. She tried to sell us some sexual favors. I don't know if she thought she would engage all four of us at once or what, but Mike asked *her* a question: May we pray for you? She was taken aback by this, but answered "Yes." We placed her in the middle of a circle and stood around her, each of us, in turn, praying a prayer of blessing over her—each man voicing a prayer on her behalf. When we said, "Amen," and looked up, she was weeping. "Would you pray for my friend, too?" she asked. "He's in desperate shape . . . dying." She stared at us in a different way now, examining us through different eyes. It was clear she had little experience with men praying for her. We prayed for her friend, as she stood, once more, in the middle of our circle, as the church's clock tower struck five. She left us asking her own questions.

When I returned to Indiana, I decided to give it a try. Open the door to questions. At church. About anything. If we have questions, why not ask them at church? Why isn't the church the first place people go when they have questions, instead of, so often, the last? I spoke with our Communications Director, Kevin Majeski, and he launched a website: *www.GoAheadAskAnything.com*. Perfectly conceived, it invited visitors to submit questions—about anything—to be answered in a sermon. If you could get an answer from a preacher, what would you ask?

A billboard campaign was also developed. Our community was blanketed with billboards, featuring the website's logo: *Go Ahead. Ask Anything.*, and over a period of 60 days, the questions poured in. Of course some members of our church posted questions, but many came from people who were in no way associated with us. Some came from nearby.

Others from far away. That's the power of the web. A search engine can be launched by someone living worlds away, in places you could not imagine, and can lead them to your website for answers.

After two months passed, the questions were sorted and grouped. Many questions were along similar lines ("How could a good God let such bad things happen?"). Others were more personal and precise ("I am pregnant. Is there a way I can determine who the father of my baby is before the baby is born? If it's my last boyfriend's baby, I don't want it and will abort it. If it is my present boyfriend's baby, I want to carry it for him . . .") Go ahead, as we said, ask anything.

We posted over four hundred questions online that surfaced during the first two months and invited web visitors to vote for ten of greatest interest to them. A web tracking system prevented multiple votes coming from the same computer. This first round of voting led to the top twenty questions. A second round of voting then took place, narrowing the top twenty to the top ten. These top ten questions, then, formed the basis of a preaching series at Madison Park. Ten questions, covering a wide variety of subjects, all of immediate interest to a world with many different takes on life but also united by the common thread of our humanity.

My commitment in answering these questions was to use the Bible as a guide. I have questioned the Bible vociferously in my lifetime and have become persuaded that it stands alone in all of literature and is, in fact, God-breathed. I know some dispute this, but it is the premise from which I wrestled with the top ten questions; it is the premise upon which this book is written.

Too often churches try to answer questions nobody is asking. *Go Ahead. Ask Anything.* at least enjoys the imprimatur of questions people *are* asking, whatever you think of the answers. It's my guess you've asked some of—if not all of—them, too.

It's been my privilege to have visited more than 50 countries. Travel has greatly stretched my horizons and brought perspective to my own world at home, as well. But I've also learned that you don't have to physically travel to expand your horizons and grow your world. You just have to be willing to ask questions. Don't be afraid of them. Seek answers, too. They can be found. For me, the Old and New Testaments are key. *Go Ahead. Ask Anything.*

Question 10

Illegal Immigration

"How should Christians respond to illegal immigration?"

This is a question I did not anticipate. When the door was opened for the public to ask anything, I imagined questions like, "Where was God when my father abused me?" or "Why didn't God heal my son of leukemia?" These are the tough, but not uncommon kind of questions posed across my pastor's desk. But illegal immigration? I must admit I did not see that one coming.

I live in Anderson, Indiana, near Indianapolis. There are 130,000 residents in our county, one of nine counties in the Indianapolis metro area that total approximately 1.8 million residents.[1] Of course, immigrants—legal and otherwise—find their way to central Indiana. But isn't this a question that roils in border states (like Arizona) or in primary points of entry to the United States (like New York)?

The truth is that even Indiana has seen an influx of people from beyond the nation's borders. Some carry documents that satisfy the law of the land, some do not. Throughout American history, there has been a dialog about immigration. We are after all, in the main, a nation of immigrants. Most Americans are descended from someone who came from somewhere else. In recent years, however, the debate has raged more intensely; it looms ever larger on the national stage; it cannot be ignored. It is front and center in many people's minds—it's certainly front and center in the headlines. It has gripped the nation's consciousness; people of every religion—or of no religion—are asking questions on the subject from one point of view or another.

The question posed by *Go Ahead. Ask Anything.* wrestles with how Christians should respond to this sea change in our culture today. And there's no question about that: it is a sea change.

According to the Pew Center of Hispanic studies, 1.6 million people entered the United States illegally in the ten years between 1980 and 1989 (see Figure 1). The number of people entering the country illegally remained fairly steady throughout that decade. But in the 1990s, the numbers began to rapidly rise. Astonishingly, in the first five years of that decade (1990–1994), the number of illegal immigrants who entered the country was two million—400,000 more than had entered in the entire preceding ten years. In the next five years, the upward trend continued—3.1 million from 1995 through 1999. Almost four million more entered from the years 2000 through 2004. The total undocumented population peaked in 2007, when an estimated 12.1 million had made their homes in the United States. From 2007-2009, the number declined slightly, to 11.1 million people. But that number is still one third higher than in 2000, and three times higher than in 1990.[2]

Figure 1

Estimates of the U.S. Unauthorized Immigrant Population by Period of Arrival, March 2008
(millions)

PERIOD	NUMBER	PERCENT
Total	11.9	100%
2005-2008	1.6	13%
2000-2004	3.7	31%
1995-1999	3.1	26%
1990-1994	2.0	16%
1980-1989	1.6	13%

Note: Estimates are based on residual methodology; see appendix. Numbers rounded independently and may not add to total shown. Estimates represent persons in the U.S. in unauthorized status as of March 2008. They do not represent the status at entry or the magnitude of unauthorized immigration during the period.

Source: Pew Hispanic Center estimates, 2008, based on March Supplements to the Current Population Survey (CPS).

Figure 1: From Jeffrey S. Passel and D'Vera Cohn. Trends in Unauthorized Immigration: Undocumented Inflow Now Trails Legal Inflow *(Washington, DC: Pew Hispanic Center, October 2008). Used by permission.*

These statistics bear witness to the astonishing increase in the sheer number of undocumented people finding their way into the United States in the last 20 years. What will be the consequence? What has been the consequence? How should Christians respond?

If this growth pattern continues, we will see huge impact. Indeed, many communities have already experienced huge impact from this trend.

Where are the undocumented immigrants from?

In 2009, the Pew Center for Hispanic Studies identified the origins of undocumented immigrants (see Figure 2). If you add up the number of people coming from Mexico and other Latin American countries, you will find 80% of the undocumented population. Principally Spanish speaking, these immigrants number 9.6 million (including some Portuguese speaking Brazilians). Eleven percent are Asian (1.32 million), 4% European or Canadian (480,000), and 4% are from Africa and other countries (480,000).[3]

Figure 2

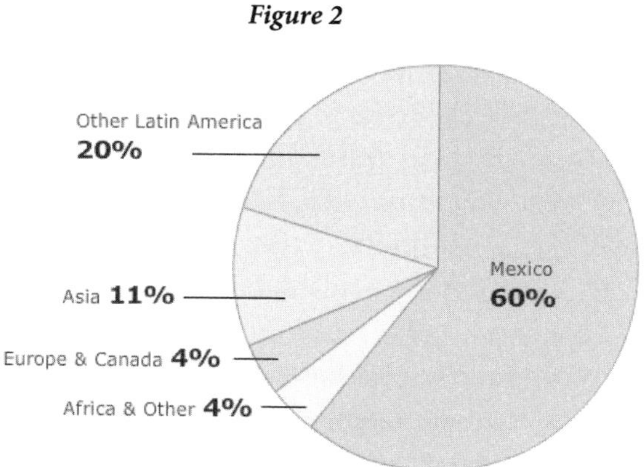

Figure 2: From Jeffrey S. Passel and D'Vera Cohn. "U.S. Unauthorized Immigration Flows Are down Sharply Since Mid-Decade" (Washington, DC: Pew Hispanic Center, October 2008). Used by permission.

What is the impact of undocumented immigrants on the economy?

Though these 11–12 million people represent less than 5% of the country's 148 million workers, they have disproportionate representation in key industries. Over one quarter of the employees in the agricultural sector, for instance, are illegal immigrants. That means one in four farm workers in the United States are living and working here illegally.[4]

I suspect that many are wringing their hands over this reality without considering the kind and quantity of labor this population provides day in and day out. People may speak against illegal immigration or in support of dramatic immigration reform, and at the same time be unaware of how they directly benefit from this work force by, for instance, purchasing produce at the local grocery. In many ways American citizens save money, celebrate value, and take for granted the relatively inexpensive access they have to fresh fruit and vegetables at the supermarket, not realizing that undocumented workers make these bargains possible. Many Americans, likewise, save money repairing their homes or find better deals on the custodial services that maintain their places of business, because immigrants, here illegally, work here. This is not an argument for the status quo; it is just an observation.

Agriculture, service industries, and construction: these industries all have disproportionate amounts of illegal immigrants employed, often for less cost than their legal counterparts. What would happen if this population were suddenly removed from the country? Some have asked, "What if we just found a way to make them disappear and reclaimed our country?"

We can only speculate, but if a quarter of the agricultural workforce did not show up for work tomorrow, there would be a serious collapse in that economic sector that would greatly and immediately impact the fresh produce aisle. The change would not make life easier for anyone on the next day, or in the next week. In fact, how many of us are willing to suddenly pay twice as much for our produce or to wait while a new agricultural work force replaces the old? Remember, we are talking about a full 25% of farm workers. Who among us would like to queue up for those farming jobs today? Remember, this challenge addresses only the food chain. Think also about service industries and construction. Ouch!

That's just placing a toe in the water, skimming the surface of this complex and multidimensional issue.

Where do the undocumented immigrants live?

The challenge of undocumented workers affects everyone in the United States. Figure 3 shows how regional impacts are disbursed. Each circle represents one of the fifty states; the larger the circle, the bigger the impact. As you can see, Indiana is not as profoundly affected as other states are, like California, Florida, Texas, or even Illinois. In some areas, the debate is more imminent, more prominent, and therefore more potent than in other areas. You can see that by this measure, Indiana, where I live, might appear to be relatively immune to this issue.[5]

On the other hand, national news networks and the Internet continue to make our world smaller and more integrated; we are more conscious than ever of the interconnectedness of not just our nation but the world. Even in a small town in Indiana illegal immigration can become a very big issue. Indeed, Indiana has a growing and dynamic community of undocumented workers, many of Hispanic origin.

The rich fabric of Hispanic culture is an increasingly prominent part of the American mosaic. Did you know there are more than 50 million Hispanic Americans today?[6] That's larger than the entire population of Canada. In the continually evolving multicultural American mix, Spanish has quickly established itself as a prominent and burgeoning language in our society, from the Cuban enclaves of Dade County and Miami, Florida, to the Latino neighborhoods of southern California to the Puerto Rican streets of New York and everywhere in between. The United States today easily has one of the top five largest Spanish-speaking populations in the world—possibly the second largest, surpassed only by Mexico.[7] Although 80% of undocumented immigrants are classified as Hispanic, that's just a fraction of the 50 million strong Hispanic community here legally (by birth, naturalization, or other government permissions to be in residence). Many people have difficulty making the distinction in their day-to-day lives. Blanket categorizations abound.

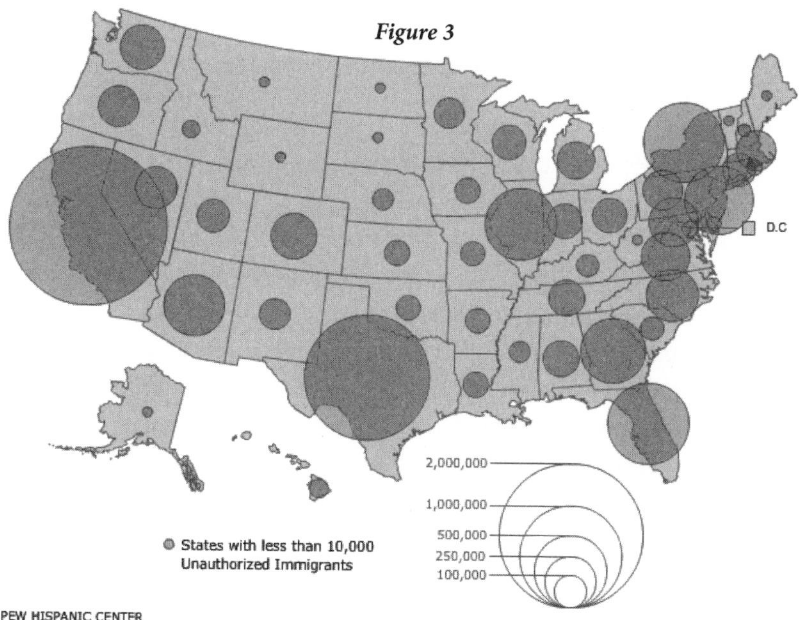

Figure 3: Jeffrey S. Passel and D'Vera Cohn. "U.S. Unauthorized Immigration Flows Are Down Sharply Since Mid-Decade," Washington, DC: Pew Hispanic Center (September 1, 2010). http://pewhispanic.org_files_report_126.pdf (accessed April 19, 2011). Used by permission.

Sometimes, we tend to stereotype or make anecdotal judgments about others based on ethnicity. This leads to all kinds of mischief and wrongdoing. It's easy to fall into these kinds of quick, prejudicial, snap judgments based on single experiences or on media exposure. People on all sides of this issue are prone to this error. As Christians, we must be very careful about discerning people's character, based not on their ethnicity but on their individual hearts and actions. Never forget, as the Scripture reminds us, God looks at and is most concerned about the heart—yours included.

There are immigrants in the United States illegally from all over the world scattered around all areas of the country. Some people may think the problem is more towering in their communities than it actually is, based on shallow ethnic stereotypes. Don't fall into that trap. It is more likely that ethnic populations within our communities are comprised of legal residents than of illegal ones. Complexion and culture are not evidence of legal status—red, yellow, black, or white. America is a land of newcomers. It always has been. And most came lawfully.

How did the undocumented immigrants get here?

What most people find surprising when I speak to this subject is that 40–50% of the people we classify as "illegal immigrants" first came into the country legally. They're illegal now because they've stayed longer than the dates assigned to their visas. They didn't just swim across the Rio Grande or jump the fence and injure a border patrol agent in Arizona. Millions came with altogether legal permission.

This means all of us must also be very careful about concluding that immigrants have all violated our borders; that is unfair and inaccurate. It also means that even if we built an impenetrable electrified fence that immobilized everyone who tried to overcome it, we still would not have addressed the five to six million people who entered the country legally but stayed illegally.[8]

The realities clothing this issue are complex, the challenges immense, the effective and functionally plausible solutions very difficult to identify.

So what?

So what? Should we, as Christians, do anything about it? Is it our problem with which to wrestle? Is it really any of our business? Shouldn't we just let somebody else take the lead and otherwise forget about it? Can we? Should we? As Christians, are we called to somehow, some way take a stand?

When faced with questions, I always turn first to the Scriptures, the word of God, the Bible. What does the Bible say about illegal immigration? Well, in some ways, not much. Like many of the questions we face in life, the Bible doesn't explicitly speak one way or another. It certainly does not say, "Build a fence, throw all the illegal immigrants out, confiscate what they leave behind, and drive their children away." It also does not say, "Accept and provide for all those who, by any means and for any purpose, find their way into your country." If you look up the words "illegal immigration" in a biblical concordance, you will not find any exact matches. The Bible does have some things to say, though.

> **Exodus 22:21**
> *"Do not oppress foreigners in any way. Remember, you yourselves were once foreigners in the land of Egypt"*

God is giving the Law to the Israelites. Moses, soon after famously parting the Red Sea and delivering the people out of Egyptian slavery, finds himself at Mount Sinai. He climbs the mountain alone and God speaks to him in a thick cloud. God blesses the nation with the Ten Commandments and then gives many other rules and regulations for the newly freed Hebrew nation. The principles they embody transcend the Old Testament era. Exodus 22:21 states one of those rules. The people had recently been freed from the slavery of a foreign power; the words were clear and clearly understood. Do not oppress foreigners. Do not be the cause of that kind of pain in anyone else's life. Remember your past and learn from it.

All of us have been outsiders at some point in life, if we stop and think about it. Christians must always be aware that they have been given opportunities they did not deserve by birth.

Leviticus 19:33-34
"Do not take advantage of foreigners who live among you in your land. Treat them like native-born Israelites, and love them as you love yourself. Remember that you were once foreigners living in the land of Egypt. I am the LORD your God."

Whenever God adds, "I am the LORD your God," at the end of a sentence, He's emphasizing: "Pay Attention. Listen up! I am the Lord. I am your God!" And what is the message we need to hear in this text? Treat foreigners, or immigrants, as you would treat one of your own. Pay them what you would pay your own. Again, remember, you were once foreigners – remember your bondage in Egypt. God takes it a step further, not just commanding that we should treat foreigners well – we should treat them as one of our own, as if they were one of us. This is a high, sometimes difficult calling. It was an extraordinary concept in the ancient world into which it was first delivered; it remains a tall mountain to climb for many followers of Jesus even today.

Deuteronomy 10:17-19
"The LORD your God is the God of gods and the Lord of lords. He is the great God, mighty and awesome, who shows no partiality and takes no bribes. He gives justice to orphans and widows. He shows love to the foreigners living among you and gives them food and clothing. You too, must show love to foreigners, for you yourselves were once foreigners in the land of Egypt."

This time God not only tells Israel to treat foreigners well, but He also explains it through example. He is the One who shows love to foreigners, giving them food and clothing. God teaches us by showing us; He models. God's heart is exposed here; this theme of caring for widows, orphans, and foreigners continues throughout the entire Bible—Old and New Testament alike. At this point in the sweeping narrative of Israel, Moses has led God's people out of Egypt, through wilderness, and to the threshold of the promised land. Forty years is a long time, and Moses reminds them of the laws God gave them years before as the exodus dawned. "Even though decades have passed, do not forget that you were once foreigners in the land of Egypt. Learn from your past and from the generations before you.

Learn from God's example." That was the message of Moses to the Israelites then; I believe it's the message of God to us now.

Matthew 25:34-35
"Then the King will say to those on the right, 'Come, you who are blessed by my Father, inherit the Kingdom prepared for you from the foundation of the world. For I was hungry and you fed me. I was thirsty, and you gave me a drink. I was a stranger, and you invited me into your home.'"

The days preceding Jesus' Passion must have been an emotional roller coaster with dramatic highs and breathtaking lows. There were huge crowds celebrating His entrance into Jerusalem through the Gate called Beautiful, waving palms as they hailed Him, "the King of Israel." Next came grim betrayal and rejection, eventually by even His closest friends. As these events unfolded, during the Passover week, Jesus talked to His followers about what it would be like when He was gone, when He returned, and what to do in the time in-between. These are some of Jesus' final instructions before He was led to die, which I think gives them special importance.

"I was a stranger, and you invited me into your home." When the disciples ask about when they have ever taken care of Jesus in this way, He responds (verse 40), "I tell you the truth, when you did it to one of the least of these my brothers and sisters, you were doing it to me."

This time the focus is not on our past (learning from our history) but on our present (considering what we are doing now). Who are the least of these for whom we need to care and feed? Could undocumented workers be among them?

Jesus speaks about His heart for those in need, those who seek help and hope. Now, juxtapose this idea against another clear teaching in the New Testament:

Romans 13:1-5
"Everyone must submit to governing authorities. For all authority comes from God, and those in positions of authority have been placed there by God. So anyone who rebels against authority is rebelling against what God has instituted, and they will be punished. For the authorities do not strike fear in people who are

> *doing right, but in those who are doing wrong. Would you like to live without fear of the authorities? Do what is right, and they will honor you. The authorities are God's servants, sent for your good. But if you are doing wrong, of course you should be afraid, for they have the power to punish you. They are God's servants, sent for the very purpose of punishing those who do what is wrong. So you must submit to them, not only to avoid punishment, but also to keep a clear conscience."*

The apostle Paul wrote this letter to Christians in Rome, which was the seat of their ancient government. They were ruled by a fairly stable governing system and, consequently, lived within a well-defined secular legal system. The Roman believers comprehended how secular law worked and had some educated opinions about how it should work. Paul wrote to them (and writes to us) in a clear and concise way: "Submit to the present authority—not only to avoid punishment, but also so you can have a clear conscience. "

When tax day approaches, when our federal income tax is due and must be filed, I'm not sure I always want to give the government my money. I work hard for what I receive, and I want to do with it what I will, including charitable giving. After all, am I not a better steward of what I have earned than the Internal Revenue Service? Okay, maybe I need to surrender some of my income to support the government, but am I required to surrender that much? This is the train of thought many taxpayers ride every April 15th. But when it comes down to it, we follow the law because it is the law, in spite of our individual views. This principle of obedience to the law, even when we do not find it easy or pleasant to do so is essential to all ordered societies.

What should we do, then, when human law directly contradicts another commandment in the Bible? When Hitler's Gestapo knocked on doors and pointed guns to compel neighbors to betray neighbors without just cause, should the law of the land have been obeyed? No. The Bible has examples of breaking the law to do good, too. Rahab housed some visitors in Jericho, violating the law of her day (see the story in Joshua). But those are exceptions to the rule, not the norm.

Reasonable laws governing orderly immigration and access to the country cannot, it seems to me, be seen as morally corrupt in themselves.

The case for disobeying them because they conflict with the higher order of God's law has never been made persuasively. The fact that many immigration laws have been ignored and unenforced has, undeniably, created some heart-breaking scenarios. But this reality must be seen in the context of failure to follow the original law in the first place, not as a rationale for further emasculating it. To continue to ignore the principle of enforcement is unlikely to produce better outcomes for anyone.

So what are the overarching lessons and themes from the Bible?

God has a heart for those who are in need.

We live in the United States, history's wealthiest civilization and we need to understand that. For instance, very few people in India could understand the validity of a PetSmart store: an entire warehouse of products dedicated to outfitting and feeding our pets. In fact, the concept of spending extra money on an animal companion that provides no service (like a goat that provides milk) is hard to comprehend in most of the developing world. Luxury is a concept wildly different from place to place. By the measure of the overwhelming mass of humanity, Americans live luxuriously.

Cars. A new car. Three or four car garages. The idea that the middle class—not the wealthiest of the wealthy—but the middle class, can live like this astounds and mystifies much of the world around us. Even in Europe. It's hard for others to understand how we consume so much of the world's resources as a routine, believing it is our birthright to do so. I wonder what Heaven thinks of our sense of entitlement and devotion to things. The desperate and appalling material need of the world around us must speak into this debate.

In the local church where I serve as pastor, we invest both at home and abroad. Ninety percent (and sometimes more) of our congregation's resources have historically been invested in our local community: a shelter for homeless women and children, an adoption agency, providing basic human needs and services, and furthering the Gospel in Anderson, Indiana, our home town. Ten percent of our resources have been shared beyond "our front door." I've had many conversations with people in my church and community about how they believe we invest too many resources, too much money, abroad.

But see the world through the eyes of villagers or street people in India or China, or go to Myanmar and find precious souls living at a subsistence level, eating roots to survive under an oppressive government that stifles initiative and opportunity. When you visit places like that (and I have), you suddenly understand that even the most economically disadvantaged neighborhoods in our country are, by most measures, far superior to those found in the rest of the world.

Does that apply to the illegal immigration question? Yes.

Those living illegally in the United States are, for the most part, here because they cannot find opportunity to better themselves in the nations of their birth. In America, the pervasive culture of opportunity to advance the cause of yourself and your family is a priceless treasure; too often taken for granted by those born here. Many people believe that if they can get a toehold for their family in the United States, future generations will call them blessed. And many illegal immigrants, working for less pay than legal residents would usually accept, live very frugally so that they can send money home to bless their loved ones.[9] Desperate poverty prompts many, who are willing to work hard and deny themselves, to assume great risks and make astonishing sacrifices for the larger good of their families.

God has a heart for people in need. And He has a heart for things that we often push aside. We think He has a heart for the Christmas spectacular at church. I believe He does, if we invest in it with the right spirit. But Jesus says that the measure by which we will be judged is directly correlated to how we help those in need. Don't imagine that your focus on standing up for the "right" kind of worship (be it liturgical, postmodern, or whatever), or in what you consider to be proper attire for a weekend worship service, or your understanding of the historical and theological debates about the synoptic gospels as compared to John's will trump your responsibility to care for the poor.

God knows you love Him by how you help those in need.

Second, God has ordained governments and nations to maintain order. Of course, despots and tyrants around the world have used the passage from Romans 13 (see page 19) to force unholy submission. But this passage cannot be fairly construed to empower evil; the Scripture endorses the place of government to advance the common good, not to defy God and oppress the vulnerable.

American culture is clothed by the notion that we are, individually, the arbiters of what is right and what is wrong. For example, many American Christians are reluctant to submit to the Body of Christ for anything, believing that they know best for themselves, that "nobody is going to tell me what to do," and that their individual opinions, ultimately, trump the wisdom of the larger community. This aspect of American culture colors Christian thinking, even in the face biblical texts that call us to defer to one another, thinking of others as better than ourselves (see Romans 12:3; Philippians 2:3). Deferring to one another and seeking the will of God as a group can lead to a more accurate understanding of the right way; when we come together to discern the truth, God can speak more clearly to us than when we are alone. Individual free agency is a God-given right; deferring to others is also a God-given responsibility.

This principle translates into cooperation with governing authorities as well, in the absence of obvious and irrefutable wrongdoing.

We are told by the Scriptures to pray for and respect those who govern us. The president of the United States, by virtue of office, merits the prayers and respect of believers, even if we profoundly disagree with policy decisions that fly from the White House. Can any of us truly comprehend the magnitude of responsibility the president must bear? Can any of us imagine for a moment a world in which our every word, our every move, and our every choice, becomes the fodder for someone else's analysis, critique or conversation? Can we not have sympathy, even if politically opposed, for the president's impossibly complex and inescapable assignment? And, cannot the same be said for those who represent us in Congress, in our state houses, governor's mansions, and more?

For all of the folly and failure of our representative government, it still is, as much as any on the planet, representative. We still live in a land where we can have a voice in our own government. American Christians, of all people, need to evaluate the moral dimensions of public policy, so let us beware of the dark and corroding cynicism of our time. Too many believers parrot their secular neighbors and whine incessantly about the perennially conniving, dishonest, manipulative, and self-aggrandizing ne'er-do-wells who govern us. This does not honor the Scriptures, our Lord, or our future.

Perhaps we should look at those who govern us as what they are: people. People with ups and downs . . . people trying to find their way . . . people who, for whatever reasons, find themselves in places of great public responsibility. There are bad apples in every barrel, of course, but most are not bad. Christians should be always thinking the best about, and calling the best out of, everyone. With this in mind, we must respect and honor, insofar as we are able by the light of Heaven, the laws they develop and bring to life.

So, if we strive to find the best in our leaders, and if we understand God's call to obey the laws of our land, and if we embrace the heart cry of God for those in need, then what should we do when government policy contravenes our mandate to care for those in need?

Some Christians have come to this conclusion: helping someone in the country illegally, while against government law, actually honors a higher law. Other Christians are not convinced any higher law is in play on this issue. And, still other believers don't care, one way or another. Here are some markers with which to, at the last, sort the positions out for yourself:

Illegal immigration is a product of economic disparity worldwide. People with opportunity at home rarely leave home for opportunities elsewhere. Perhaps you've seen the T-shirt that pictures some Native Americans with angry expressions on their faces and fire in their eyes, holding various weapons, ready to attack. The caption reads, "Fighting illegal immigration since 1492." Think about how Europeans came to the Americas in the first place. They came because of the lack of opportunities for advancement in their land or origin.

The solution, then, surely includes helping the world escape the chains of poverty.

"That's impossible," you say. "There is no way that can happen."

It is not impossible. Yes, it can happen: one person, one village, one place at a time. The India Gospel League—the organization that led me to my trip to India, which ultimately inspired the *Go Ahead. Ask Anything.* series—is eradicating hopeless poverty every single day. I've traveled extensively and have rarely seen a transformational ministry as effective as this one, preaching the Gospel, redeeming souls, and meeting both spiritual and physical needs. This Indian-run organization walks into villages steeped in poverty and does two key things: 1) they preach Jesus Christ as Lord, introducing villagers to completely new concepts about their Creator and themselves, and 2) they build, what they call Life Centers in the villages. The Life Center is often the only stable, permanent structure in the area. It's not elaborate, just an open room with concrete walls and a cement floor. It can fit usually accommodate 100–150 people at one time. It becomes the church's meetinghouse for the village. It becomes the school. It's the place where basic needs are met, such as dental care and hygiene. And as the people respond to the opportunities presented in the Life Center, more resources are attracted to help develop the local economy. A goat is loaned to an aspiring businesswomen's cooperative, providing milk. Microloans provide the seed for new enterprises. Literacy grows. The status of women is elevated. Hope is born and nourished, for new days and a better life. God is discovered personally and not simply imagined as a passive, distant, and capricious deity. Business opportunities appear where previously there were none. This is an elementary—and yet empowering—example of what is being done, what can be done, anywhere.

People need help. Our spiritual calling throughout the Old and New Testaments is to help those in need. The India Gospel League does just that, all under the banner of Jesus Christ. Nearly 70,000 villages in rural India are being transformed in this way as I write.[10] Ministries like this around the world need our support—not just our moral support, but our dollars, advocacy, and prayers, too. The dots connect very powerfully to the challenges of immigration across national borders.

We cannot say, "I don't want those people to come to my country," and, at the same time say, "I want to ignore the world's suffering; it's none of my business or it's impossible for me to address." Such an approach is doomed to fail and frustrate; it does not problem-solve. You may as well stand before the ocean and command its waves to stop.

Can we alone eradicate poverty around the world? No. But we can change one life, or one town, or one church's life somewhere in the world. Sign up with an organization like the India Gospel League and do something now to help people where they live now. It's a necessary part of a Christian response to illegal immigration.

But wait a minute, you think: that's not enough. I have to vote for a president, engage my senators, deal with undocumented workers at my workplace or in my hometown. What can I do here at home?

Everyone has a story. You do. I do. The undocumented worker does. You can look at this problem with a broad, bird's eye view, or you can look at it one person at a time, one story at a time.

When I try to help someone, an individual or a family, whatever the need, I have to stop and ask, "Am I really helping them, or am I simply prolonging their suffering?" How do I really help?

I visited India for the first time in 1987. I was unprepared for all that I would experience on that trip; I had never been to the developing world before. I walked off the plane in Mumbai expecting to see magnificent palaces built for moguls and maharajahs mixed with some poverty and a lot of British-Indian accents. I had no idea. There is spectacular architecture, of course, and a rich tapestry of culture, but the poverty and desperation of millions on the street took my breath away. I wanted to give away all that I had, in the moment, on my first venture outside the flat in which I stayed.

Standing at 6'2" with light brown hair, blue eyes, and wearing Banana Republic cargo pants and shirt, I was very conspicuous as a westerner in a sea of shorter, darker-skinned, dress-very-differently Indians on the street. A crowd, seeing a westerner inside, rushed my cab at an intersection.

Suddenly, a man appeared at the window. His face was disfigured. The only thing I could think was that he had suffered some awful accident or assault. The bone of his nose had been exposed by some kind of tear to his flesh, and it was framed by dried blood. His hands were nubbed, as he thrust them toward me through the open cab window. His eyes begged for help as he spoke in a language I did not know but understood perfectly: "Please, please, can you give me something?"

Stunned, I reached for my wallet and instinctively began to pull out some cash. The taxi driver reached across the seat and slapped my hands down. "Leper," he mumbled and immediately began pushing the man's hands back and, and the same time, manually trying to roll up the back window where I was seated.

"What are you doing!?" he scolded me. "If you, a white man, give him any money, within minutes there will be hundreds of them here, trying to get your money. You'll start a riot, they will overturn the car, and we will both be left with nothing. And they will not be helped!" He was intense, determined, and direct—I was quite taken aback. I was just trying to help.

What did I learn? After a few days in India I understood that my visceral reaction to human need, my first response to simply dole money out in the moment, might make me feel better but did not provide real help to anyone. I would simply waste precious resources and perpetuate hopelessness with evaporating remedies. I learned it was better to help strategically, partnering with organizations that could affect real, positive change. For the lepers of India. For everyone. I emptied my wallet later, investing in relief charities like the India Gospel League (which addresses the needs of lepers and their families with long-term solutions).

This same lesson can help us address the tragedies of illegal immigration.

The Questions: Is breaking the law to give an immigrant a chance in the United States really helping them—helping anyone—or does it simply prolong suffering and despair? Am I doing something to feel good in the moment that does not actually help over the long haul? Be sure that when you choose to act you do so only after careful prayer and thoughtful assessment; be sure that what you do really does help to solve not just surface problems but root causes.

My Answer: I believe helping illegal immigrants must be done within a legal framework. If faced with someone who is in the country illegally, I would have to seek legal counsel for them, or least attempt to build bridges to do so. I believe, in many cases, in the end, that will require repatriation to the country of origin; I may find myself helping them find a way back home if there is not place they can legally remain in the United States.

I cannot help anyone in this scenario by breaking or by ignoring the law. Doing so will only perpetuate the need and will condemn the very ones I seek to help to live "under cover," hiding from the law. Living in the country illegally denies them redress when wronged (because of fear of discovery in the legal system), makes them more vulnerable to abuse (again, because ordinary legal remedies are not available), forces them to live always looking over their shoulders, and creates stress and tension for a lifetime. Healthcare. Education. Credit. Legal protections. All of these are compromised for illegal immigrants. How can enabling such an outcome be kind or loving?

If I have an opportunity to help someone who is in the country illegally, I could stand up, do the homework, and take action. If that means they need to be deported, then I need to help them beyond taking them to the border. I need to help them once they get home. If God places you in the company of undocumented individuals, then you need to make an ongoing commitment to help them—not by breaking the law, but by working within the framework of the law.

But what about those laws? Don't we live in a society where the law is fluid, always being debated and checked for fairness? Do the laws need to be changed? Yes.

We are obviously living in a broken situation. The illegal immigration problem continues to escalate. The number of undocumented workers in this country has decreased slightly over the past few years, but over the past 30 years it has clearly grown. I think it's very important for us to prayerfully seek out political candidates who offer honest compassionate, transformational approaches to this issue. Ask God to help you find these candidates. Find someone who understands that simply building a wall is not going to solve the problem. Find somebody who has a heart, who understands the need to provide stable and secure borders, and who comprehends the need for a comprehensive solution (including economic development beyond our borders).

Pray. Learn. Listen. Think. Act. For Jesus' sake.

Chapter 9

God: The Decider?

"Does God decide who gets hurt, who suffers, who gets a pass on suffering, who gets sick, and who doesn't?"

Randy Kerr and I have a lot in common.[1] He moved from the West Coast to become a pastor in Indiana, just like me. He was born in Seattle, just like me. And, his mother by birth wasn't able to care for him, so she relinquished him for adoption, just like me. He knows what I know: that parents aren't always defined by blood, but by love instead—and that the dad and mom who adopted him, gave him their name, and poured their lives into him, *are* his parents, in the most wonderful way. Like me, he grew up in Washington State (although in Vancouver, across the Columbia River from Portland, Oregon; my adopted family remained in Seattle). Yes, Randy and I share much in common.

As a young man, Randy found a job—and a career—with United Parcel Service, UPS (you know, "Brown"). As an adult, he also found his way into a local church, discovered the Gospel in a life-changing way, began investing in the children's ministry, and then in the youth and young adult programs. He is the kind of guy who inevitably would end up on stage telling stories in church or reading the Scripture during a Sunday morning service. Along the way, pastors and lay leaders in the church began to recognize a ministerial gift in him; in time, after many years, a staff position in his local church opened and he was invited to step into the role. Ultimately, he walked away from UPS and became a pastor, full-time, in the only church he had ever known.

To receive a call to the pastoral ministry and remain in the church in which you have been raised in the faith and taken a seat in the pews, is rare. It's hard, sometimes, for fellow members of your congregation to sit next to you in the pew one day and then follow you as a shepherd the next. It takes a unique move of the Spirit Himself. It's unique, but not altogether one-of-a-kind. It's also my story.

I became the pastor of the church in which I was raised, too. I left a promising job (that I loved!) at Northwest Airlines to become a pastor. My church family recognized in me something I did not: a pastoral gift. They called it out of me and invited me to become their pastor. It was the Lord's doing—it had to be.

That's Randy's story. And mine, too. Our experiences are so similar that it is no wonder that our friendship is deep, unwavering.

Randy married Tamara, and together they had a son (Reid) and a daughter (Samantha). A few years ago, Randy sensed a calling from God to walk away from the safety and security—the comfort and familiarity—of Washington, of Vancouver, of his church and his extended family—all he'd ever really known. He felt a call to move to Indiana.

Again, I've been there, done that, too. I also found myself wrestling with God, some years before Randy, to move away from everything I knew and loved in Seattle and start a new life in the heartland, in Indiana. Like Randy, an only child adopted at birth with a transcendent sense of responsibility to my parents, as well as my wife and children, I could not escape the truth that God was moving me 2,500 miles away.

Randy and I both needed to take a chance and trust God in new, more challenging ways. We are both men committed to "doing the right thing" and making choices for our families that we believe will please Heaven. Interestingly, we did not know each other at all until I had already left Seattle and relocated across the continent. It was not until just before Randy moved to South Bend that we met.

Randy and Tamara packed up the car and moved to Hoosierland with their son (then still in high school), leaving Samantha (grown now and with a life of her own), behind in the Pacific Northwest. Uprooting a teenaged son close to graduating from high school can be challenge, but Reid made the adjustment and worked hard to give it a go. Being separated from their daughter by thousands of miles was a stretch, too, but they remained close and communicated often.

They arrived in midwinter and found South Bend buried in a lake-effect blizzard. Blinding snow, the broad level landscape of Indiana, cornfields and trees-without-leaves, chicken-with-noodles-heaped-over-mashed-potatoes-and-gravy: the Kerrs quickly realized they were a long, long way from the temperate climate, evergreen trees, dramatic mountains, and lean cuisine of the Pacific Northwest. But Randy and his family believed they were doing the right thing; God had called them to love and live in Indiana.

Another one of the challenges posed by this move was being distanced from Randy's parents. Randy is their only son; Reid their only grandson. Not long after settling into South Bend, Reid flew back to Portland to visit with his grandparents and the world he had left behind. Randy's parents drove to the airport to meet their grandson and pulled their car along the curb outside the passenger pick-up area. Randy's mom pulled the car into a space and put it in park. She stepped out onto the walk to search for Reid and Randy's dad slid across the seat to get behind the wheel (so he could conform to the security regime all airports enforce on waiting cars these days). As he moved from the passenger seat to the driver's seat, though, he accidentally shifted the car into gear. Immediately realizing what had happened, he slammed his foot on the brake.

But Randy's dad missed the brake pedal and hit the accelerator pedal instead.

The car lurched forward and triggered a chain reaction which crushed a pedestrian—a young Oregon physician, married with young children—loading luggage into the trunk of his car ahead. His legs were horribly smashed, pinned between the front and rear bumpers of two cars. Reid had just stepped outside of the terminal and witnessed the whole terrifying scene. The crash. The cries. The pain. The innocent victim. The victim's family. His grandparents. Agonizing. The horror of it all.

And the questions: Did God orchestrate these events? Did He decide that Randy's parents would be at the center of this tragedy's cause? Did He mark the young physician as a victim, in advance? Is it the will of Heaven that this gifted young doctor would lose the use of his legs? And that every person involved would suffer grief in some way? Was it God's design that moved Randy to Indiana, prompted his son to fly home that day, and set Randy's parents up for the fateful curbside pick-up, while at the same time, arranging the victim's trajectory to guarantee he would be the one struck?

Should God be blamed for calling Randy to Indiana in the first place? If Randy had not moved, he could better care for his parents close to home and this awful turn of events would be the stuff of a Hollywood film, not real life. If only. If only we . . . No, if only God: yes, if only God had not initiated the train of events. This is where our minds wander when we attempt to come to terms with events beyond our control.

Randy did what he could to be a healing touch, before leaving his parents in Vancouver and return to Indiana. They were, as was everyone involved, emotionally distraught, dressed by grief alone. He helped them get started on the insurance claims, prepare for the legal implications, and cope with the stress. He had to be strong for them, but, of course, was shaken to the core inside of himself, too.

Randy flew back to Indiana, arriving late in the evening. He drove home from the airport in South Bend, dropped his bags by the door, and collapsed into his bed. The phone rang. He answered the phone and heard what every parent fears most: his daughter was dead, her life tragically lost in a traffic accident.

What?

It cannot be. Impossible. Unbelievable. No! No! After all, Randy had just walked into his house, after the harrowing ordeal in Portland; a young doctor is crippled, his parents are a wreck, he feels responsible, as their only son, to care for them, but he's been moved—by God, mind you—thousands of miles away—and now his only daughter is dead? It was another freak car accident. A semi loaded with large cylindrical pipes swerved on the highway, throwing one of the pipes into the windshield of his daughter's car, claiming her life in minutes.

Is God the author of these events? Did He arrange for Samantha to die—and to die in this way?

Did God choose for Randy, Tamara, and Reid—now their only child surviving—to endure this loss, as well, and on the heels of the airport mayhem days before? On the other hand, did God choose for me to have four sons who have all grown up strong and tall, finding their way through life in good health and able-bodied? Did God choose for my parents to escape the moment Randy's parents have faced? And, has God chosen that only the young doctor in Portland would have his legs crushed, while I am jogging six miles a day?

Did God choose for you to stay close to home, to be near your friends and friends for a lifetime, while others must be uprooted and condemned to live in a refugee camp because of trouble in their homeland? Did He destine you to live on high ground while someone else was born to be swept away in a tsunami?

Does God cause some people to make right choices and suffer along the way, nonetheless, while others make wrong choices and seem to sail along above the fray?

These are the big questions of life, important questions. And if we're honest, we all have to admit that we wrestle with them.

I have another long-time friend in Seattle, Howard Owens.[2] Howard was a student at the University of Washington who, just out of curiosity, walked into our church one day. He loved it, dedicated himself to Christ, and became a part of our church family. He graduated and became a Boeing engineer. Brilliant, handsome, athletic, fun, gentle and strong, both at once, Howard is one of the best men I know. When Howard and I were both in our 20's (yes, that's been a few years ago), I learned to admire and respect him immensely. I still do. Nobody's perfect, as they say, but Howard comes as close as anyone who has crossed my path.

Howard's father, John, was not so long ago diagnosed with Parkinson's, a dreadful disease that compromises so much in life. Howard's mother, Janet, visited her husband every day in the assisted living community in suburban Seattle in which he eventually had to live. She was devoted to him—and her family. John Owens, like Howard, had been a Boeing engineer, brilliant and successful by every measure of this world. Janet was, even after her husband's illness, elegant and poised, gracious and striking in an understated but inescapable way. Some years after Howard found his way into the Lord's arms, so did Janet, and she loved being a part of their church family, as well.

One day, Janet Owens, disappeared. She was supposed to meet her grandson, Kevin, (Howard's son) at his house, but didn't show. Kevin called Howard and said Janet didn't come and didn't answer her phone.

After making some calls, Howard discovered that Janet's car was in the parking lot of his father's assisted-living center. He left work and immediately drove there. She had come to share lunch with her husband, signed in at the desk, as usual, and then signed out shortly thereafter. But, her car was still there. She was not. Very strange.

The police were called. They were able to unlock her car and found her purse. Her wallet was not in her purse, though. Howard and his wife, Kathy, stood by watching, intuitively fearing something terrible had happened. People of profound faith, they prayed, desperately.

Police search teams were called in, scouring the area, the wooded ravine nearby. None of Janet's friends or family or the resident staff in the assisted living center had heard from or seen Janet since lunch. Only her car was in view. Hours passed. No sign of her anywhere.

Eventually, as the afternoon darkened and evening's shadows appeared, after all of the searching and calling out of her name, someone thought to open the trunk of Jane's car. Inside the trunk of her car, still in the assisted living center's parking lot, was found the body of Janet Owens. Dead.

How can it be? How can it be? No. No. Impossible! How could this happen to Howard? Not Howard! Not good, kind, strong, thoughtful Howard!

And then, in the coming weeks, blood was discovered under Janet's fingernails, indicating a struggle. Of course, dead bodies are not stuffed into automobile trunks unless a crime has been committed. The blood DNA evidence would match that of a young man employed by the assisted living center, who was actually assigned to care for John Owens; charges were filed, alleging that this staff member had stolen Janet's wallet, strangled her, placed her body in the trunk, and escaped through the wooded ravine adjacent to the parking lot. The accused was, after a long delay and trial, convicted of Jane Owen's murder; he is in prison now.

Again, the question comes. Did God mark Howard Owens to lose his mother this way? Was Janet marked by Heaven for tragedy? Unspeakable and unnecessary tragedy?

If there is a God, was I chosen for this? And why?

I do not presume to have all knowledge; I do not mean to appear pretentious in even attempting to answer the question. It is a question, after all, with which the greatest minds and souls of the ages have wrestled, over time. But, the Word of God is a trustworthy and inspired sourcebook with answers for the world's even most intractable and difficult questions.

Within the Bible's collection of 66 books, Job most famously approaches the query. Job suffers. He's a good man who suffers. And, as the book that bears his name opens, we are given a glimpse of the way this world really works; a veil is lifted.

Job 1:6-12
"One day the members of the heavenly court came to present themselves before the Lord, and the Accuser, Satan, came with them. 'Where have you come from?' the Lord asked Satan. Satan answered the Lord, 'I have been patrolling the earth, watching everything that's going on.' Then the Lord asked Satan, 'Have you noticed my servant Job? He is the finest man in all the earth. He is blameless—a man of complete integrity. He fears God and stays away from evil.' Satan replied to the Lord, 'Yes, but Job has good reason to fear God. You have always put a wall of protection around him and his home and his property. You have made him prosper in everything he does. Look how rich he is! But reach out and take away everything he has, and he will surely curse you to your face!' 'All right, you may test him,' the Lord said to Satan. 'Do whatever you want with everything he possesses, but don't harm him physically.' So Satan left the Lord's presence."

First, notice that there is a kind of court in Heaven, which is constantly in session, presided over by a judge, a Sovereign, Who never sleeps. Interestingly, Satan--a distinct, defined, individual persona throughout the Scripture—has some mysterious access to this courtroom, in which he intersects with God. Satan is a name that literally means "the adversary," and here he is also called "the accuser." He has other biblical names, too (e.g. "the prince of power of this world" and "the father of all lies"), and is in some very significant ways in command of the creation God originally termed "good." Satan is patrolling and moving in our world, even now, just as he was in Job's day.

God describes this one man, Job, as a man of *integrity*. The English word integrity derives from the same Latin word from which we find "integer," as in a whole number. We want to be integers, whole numbers—not piece-meal, not broken, but complete and whole. Job fears God and avoids evil, he is an integer, he is whole, consistent; he has integrity.

While we're here on earth, right now as you are reading this book or listening to this message, wherever you are, whoever you are, there is a hearing in process in a parallel universe; Heaven's courtroom is in session and cases are being considered, accusations are being made, and outcomes, here below, are in play.

And guess what? God is noticing how we conduct ourselves; Satan is, too. Both are interested in who we are and what we become.

What we read next describes the way that Job is tested. He loses everything he owns, all his possessions, his wealth, even his family. His children all tragically die. And when Job gets the news that everything is gone, he reacts in this way:

> **Job 1:20-22**
> *"Job stood up and tore his robe in grief. Then he shaved his head and fell to the ground to worship. He said,*
>
> *'I came naked from my mother's womb,*
> *and I will be naked when I leave.*
> *The LORD gave me what I had,*
> *and the LORD has taken it away.*
> *Praise the name of the LORD!'*
>
> *In all of this, Job did not sin by blaming God."*

So, lesson number one: our God is great, He is powerful, and He is good. Satan has power, too, but power wielded to do us harm.

Job is a man of God and God knows it. Satan also knows it and, consequently, wants to cause him grief. The text suggests that Satan's ambition is not so much to injure Job as it is to prove God's view of Job wrong. Ultimately, Satan's interest in Job is subordinate to his argument with God. Satan is contesting with God for supremacy; wounding God's people is a way of assaulting God. Satan may find satisfaction in feeding off the misery of good people like Job, but it is more likely, in my view, that he finds greater dark pleasure in imagining God's sense of loss if Job can be turned against his Maker.

This much seems clear, throughout Scripture: if the object is to see God grieve, injure one of His children. Satan knows this and demands God allow him to prove Job's fidelity is not simply a result of God's protection.

With this line of reasoning, then, it is Satan who has Job in his sights. It is Satan who is the author of his misery and the tragedies that rob Job of so much. These losses are not Heaven-sent but hell-bent.

To be fair, Job does say, "The Lord gives and the Lord takes away." We and Job both know God gives every good and perfect gift. It's quite natural then, for Job to reason that if God gives perfect gifts then it must also be God who takes them away. But in the end, Job does not understand what's going on in Heaven's court. As he speaks, he has not been able to see what we can see. Job had not seen the veil lifted by the revelation of God's Word in the way we can now, even though that revelation frames the book that bears his name and tells his story. Job comes to terms with his losses without the benefit of the book of Job.

This makes Job's attitude all the more remarkable and a very healthy and life-giving approach from which we can all learn something. If I were to summarize Job's response to his losses—to the question, "Does God decide who gets hurt, etc.?"—my paraphrase would go like this: "You know what? I've received some amazing gifts in life and experienced some wonderful moments; I've been blessed in ways I did not deserve. I'm so thankful for these gifts, each one, even if I had them only for a little while. Now they are gone. Whatever comes and goes, I know my God will provide for me."

Job does not curse God, as his wife later encourages him to do, because he is convinced—he chooses to believe—that God is good.

Or course, the troubling part of this theology and systematic frame of reference is that God allows Satan to test us in these awful ways. It could be reasonably argued that because God allows these tragedies that he is also responsible for them. Still, I am not persuaded.

If I allow you to get in my car and ask you to wear a seatbelt but you refuse, am I responsible for injuries you sustain if we are in an accident? I knew traveling without a seatbelt would greatly exaggerate your chances of injury (or even death), but I did not compel you to be prudent, either. Would you say I caused your injuries because I allowed you to be exposed to them?

If I purchase a ticket for you to fly to Paris, and the plane subsequently has mechanical difficulties and goes down, am I responsible for your death? If I had not placed you in the situation—and there was no way you could have purchased the ticket yourself—you would never have been exposed to such risks. Were the risks reasonable? Yes. Did you choose to fly? Yes. Is it reasonable to choose life and live in this broken world? Yes. Are there profound risks? Yes. Because God has allowed us to live, because He has brought us to life, even as the "devil prowls about seeking whom he may devour" (see 1 Peter 5:8), is God responsible for the injuries we sustain by the devil's hand?

Allowance is not the same as causation. The best we can do is acknowledge that God sometimes *allows* us to suffer. That is a long way from God *deciding* "who gets hurt."

As that allowance is made, though, God nevertheless governs the parameters of what Satan can do. Satan may originate the disaster; God establishes the boundaries. Why does God allow the disasters? We may never in this life know. But does God choose those on whom the disaster falls? Not through the lens of Job's story. Satan makes the call.

The Bible does refer to some plagues and troubles sent by God as judgments. These, however, fall within the realm of the "reap as you sow" principle. "Don't be misled—you cannot mock the justice of God. You will always harvest what you plant" (Galatians 6:7). There is a law of reciprocity at work in the moral order of the universe that leads sometimes to grief. If you are unforgiving, for instance, you will be unforgiven. But the questions posed in this section are not about earned trouble—difficulties and challenges we know we deserve because we have made foolish and even sinful choices in life. We can all understand the discipline of loss in cases like those.

The more problematic issue is the notion of innocents injured, tragedy underserved. This is the stuff of Job.

James 1:2-8

"Dear brothers and sisters, when troubles come your way, consider it an opportunity for great joy. For you know that when your faith is tested, your endurance has a chance to grow. So let it grow, for when your endurance is fully developed, you will be perfect and complete, needing nothing.

"If you need wisdom, ask our generous God, and he will give it to you. He will not rebuke you for asking. But when you ask him, be sure that your faith is in God alone. Do not waver, for a person with divided loyalty is as unsettled as a wave of the sea that is blown and tossed by the wind. Such people should not expect to receive anything from the Lord. Their loyalty is divided between God and the world, and they are unstable in everything they do."

Troubles come our way. That's the way of this world. Until the Lord returns to make all things right and restore Eden's day—until the enemy of our souls, the adversary, Satan, is, at last, taken out—joy and beauty will be mixed with grief and brokenness.

But, even in trouble, believe in joy, because God is for you, not against you. Perfection, wholeness—becoming an integer—is found along this pathway. The question is not whether or not God marked you for trouble or blessing, but, instead, how does God want you to triumph in the face of your challenges?

My wife, reflecting upon her own losses over time (including surviving clergy sexual abuse and later being raped as a student at the University of Washington) drew this lesson from the book of Job. She said she had learned not to ask God, "Why me?" but, instead, "Use me." How can God use me even if Satan himself has robbed me? She's sharp. And a survivor.[3]

> **Genesis 50:19-20**
> *"But Joseph replied, 'Don't be afraid of me. Am I God, that I can punish you? You intended to harm me, but God intended it all for good. He brought me to this position so I could save the lives of many people."*

If ever there were a narrative of trial and tribulation, it's Joseph's. His brothers kidnap him, plot to kill him, and ultimately sell him into slavery. From there his life becomes a roller coaster of extreme ups and downs. He's enslaved, he's honored, he's falsely accused of a horrific crime, he's jailed, he's rescued, he's honored again, and so on. In time, he rises to power in Egypt, and the same brothers who once sought to destroy him now must seek his help.

In reply, Joseph articulates a fundamental truth: What they intended for harm, God turned for the good. What the devil intends to rob, the Lord turns to redeem.

Don't blame God because Joseph's brothers were sad, pathetic, jealous losers. And don't blame God because Potiphar's wife was a lonely woman with no self-control and low self-esteem. Don't blame God for their weaknesses.

Apart from self-induced suffering, there are two kinds of pain we encounter in life. There's the apparent random disaster—a tsunami or tornado, a pipe on a truck loosened from its fitting and crashing through a windshield. These disasters are born in a creation corrupted by sin, a once-perfect world now broken, not working flawlessly as God once designed. Randy Kerr and Job both know about this.

There's another kind of pain born in the twisted corners of the human heart, in which deliberate harm is done without cause—blowing up passengers on an airplane to make a political point, for instance, or false accusations inspired by jealousy or disappointment—or even murdering a gentle soul for the sake of her wallet. Joseph and Howard Owens know about this.

Whichever these two kinds of pain you experience, know that God is not the cause; He has not chosen you to receive it. It is the devil's business.

God chooses to work all things (even the tough stuff) together for the good, for those who are called by Him and love Him. Each of the people I have named in this chapter: Randy, Job, Howard, Joseph, my wife—have heard God's call and accepted it.

In the face of hurt, the question of choice, then, is not so much about God's choices as our own. Choose to surrender into God's loving care and what Satan means for harm, God will turn for good. In your life. In your world.

> **Romans 8:35-39**
> *"Can anything ever separate us from Christ's love? Does it mean he no longer loves us if we have trouble or calamity, or are persecuted, or hungry, or destitute, or in danger, or threatened with death? No, despite all these things, overwhelming victory is ours through Christ, who loved us.*
>
> *"And I am convinced that nothing can ever separate us from God's love. Neither death nor life, neither angels nor demons, neither our fears for today nor our worries about tomorrow—not even the powers of hell can separate us from God's love. No power from the sky above or in the earth below—indeed, nothing in all creation will ever be able to separate us from the love of God that is revealed in Christ Jesus our Lord."*

When I talked to Randy Kerr on the day of his daughter's death, he howled. He wept. He cried out. He called me while sitting on a plane, after having just landed to pick up the body of his precious daughter; he cried out and said he didn't know if he could go on. He didn't know if he could do anything. All I knew to say was that he only had to make it through that day. You just have to make it through today.

And when he went to the coroner and was told that the face of his daughter was so badly mangled in the accident that it was beyond recognition, his only reaction was to hold his wife and sob, uncontrollably, because he knew he would never be able to say good-bye to his little girl, as he had hoped; he would never be able to see her face again.

Just keep pushing through today.

And then he had to decide what to do next. He and his wife decided to hold a memorial service for Samantha at her home church in Vancouver. It was so difficult to stand there, sit there, grieve there, even though it was home. Just one day at a time.

And then what?

In the weeks, months, and years since her passing, Randy and Tamara Kerr have heard countless stories of positive life change because of their daughter's consistent commitment to God and loving witness. She chose to let God work for the good in her and it impacted a world beyond the imagination of her family and friends.

Randy has not blamed God for Samantha's death. He explained to me that he believes his daughter is with God, in a place where she is complete and perfect, whole. And even though he, like Job, has suffered loss beyond words, he, like Job has remained holy and blameless in the way he has trusted God, even in the valley of hard questions.

And what about you? How will you choose to react to what the devil chooses to do? Will you fix blame at his feet, or at God's? It isn't God who decides what in your life will be broken—that's the Devil's business. God's choice is to help restore and redeem even what the devil has taken.

When you have trouble remembering this, remember the Cross. Satan's fingerprints are all over the tree upon which Jesus was hung to die; the death of Jesus was the most excruciating, humiliating, agonizing at every level, death that could be conceived. How could it be? How cold the crime, how merciless the perpetrator? Who decided?

Yet somehow, incredibly, the Cross, held in the Hand of God, has become the most pervasive emblem of hope the world has ever known—not just any cross, but the Cross of Christ. And the world has never been the same.

Life is not easy. For anyone. We all have mountains to climb and burdens to bear, but God has you marked for the good.

Today I do not know what circumstances you face. I do not know if you have been wounded like Randy or Job—or maybe injured like Howard or Joseph. I do not know what trials you may have faced or must still overcome. Maybe you have been so desperate that you have, like Jesus, fairly cried out, "My God, my God, why have your forsaken me?"[4]

But, whatever the difficulty, no matter how dark the night or hopeless the hour, know that God's choice for you is peace and life, not misery. He has a plan for you that Satan himself cannot destroy, if you will surrender into His will. You can make it. One day at a time.

When hurt overwhelms us, the question must not be, "Did God decide I should hurt?" but should be, "What will I decide to do in the face of Satan's attempt to steal, rob, and destroy? How can I align my heart with God's and find His way forward?"

The choice, then, is ours.

Question 8

Sex, Church and Straight Talk

"Given the damage that Satan causes through sexual temptation, why is the church so reluctant to preach about strategies to avoid lust, premarital sex, and Internet pornography?"

I know exactly when and where I was when it happened. I was traveling from Indianapolis to Asheville, North Carolina, on US Air, connecting through Charlotte. It was October, and I was flying to speak at the Billy Graham Training Center at The Cove at a retreat hosted by Christians Broadcasting Hope (CBH). The Cove is one of the most extraordinary places on the planet—a spectacular property nestled in a forested ravine of the Blue Ridge Mountains, especially glorious in autumn, as the steep hillsides are painted red and orange. I am the on-air host for a weekly radio program called *ViewPoint*, heard globally under the umbrella of CBH. In this role, it is my privilege to teach at the CBH Retreat each year, enjoying the company of hundreds of the broadcast's listeners and friends. They gather from coast-to-coast to search the Scriptures, pray, listen, learn and take a deep breath in the gorgeous facilities and breathtaking landscape that are The Cove.

Running late, I ran to the gate, briefcase, jacket and tie flying in my wake. At last—and as the last passenger—I walked down the jet way to find my seat.

Everyone else was seated already; I found my place, near the front of economy on the aisle and tossed my laptop into the overhead compartment, pulling a Time magazine out for the ride. The jet was a MD80 model, with two seats on one side of the aisle and three on the other. I believe I was in 5B, with a young, 20-something blond woman in 5A, next to the window.

As I hurried to buckle up and settle down after the harried run to the gate, I noticed that my seatmate was wrapped in a blanket from the neck down, leaning against the window. Her eyes were closed. She had a very fair complexion, but her cheeks were unusually rosy, flushed even, as if struggling with a fever of some kind.

"Great," I thought to myself, selfishly, of course. "I'm seated next to Typhoid Mary." I leaned toward the aisle and away from the seemingly afflicted. Dr. Lyon had no time for her germs. Airplane cabins are bad enough under the best of circumstances, breeding grounds for who-knows-what-kind-of-recycled-airborne-infections—and now I've been placed next to the plague. Petty? Self-absorbed? Yes, I'm sorry to admit, but that was my wretched attitude that day. And I was on my way to teach *others* about the Gospel of Jesus!

I remembered reading somewhere that breathing through your nose helps filter airborne germs out of the oxygen passed to your lungs. Breathing through your mouth was like a germ-vacuum. I'm a runner and tend to breathe through my mouth unconsciously sometimes, especially if I get drowsy (like on planes). I worked very intentionally to keep my mouth closed and breathe through my nose. As I settled down into my seat, all these ideas flew through my head, and I realized that I was breathing quite heavily in the first few moments. I tried to be as quiet as possible, fearful that I might wake her up. What if she started a conversation with me and spewed her toxic breath toward me? What an idiot! Yes, I mean me.

We taxied to the runway, took off, and climbed to cruising altitude. I buried myself in my *Time* magazine. Typhoid Mary was motionless and never stirred. The flight attendants came and went with Coke and peanuts; 5A never moved. Every now and then I would remember my predicament and get frustrated in that kind of I'm-trapped-on-this-plane sort of way frequent travelers sometimes do, looking at my watch to calculate how much longer I'd have to breathe through my nose before I could escape and drink in a deep breath through my mouth.

After an hour or so in the air, 5A came to life. She sat up, the blanket dropped to her waist, she tussled her long blond hair, and looked toward me. I tried not to look, still leaning into the aisle. Her germ-laden fingers touched my sleeve, and she leaned toward me to speak. My worst fears realized.

She suddenly seemed not so sick as I had thought and quite attractive.

"Do you know about sex?" she asked quietly.

I froze. What? What kind of question is that? She spoke deliberately, carefully, in a kind of a hushed tone. I tried to act as if I did not notice her question, even though her hand had gestured for my attention as she tapped on my sleeve.

"Do you know about sex?" She asked again, somewhat impatiently, as if she were perturbed that I did not answer immediately. "What's up with this girl?" I thought to myself, still trying to imagine how I could appropriately reply. What possible response could I make and maintain some sense of dignity—you know, that whole gentleman deal that some guys (like me) aspire to own.

She sat even more upright, stared directly at me, and said for a third time, coldly, "Do you know about sex?!" It felt almost as much a command as a question.

Exasperated, embarrassed, and cornered I decided that the best response would be to employ active listening. Active listening, of course, is the process by which one person restates what he thinks he has heard to help reassure the other that she is being heard and understood. It does not necessarily give an answer, but it acknowledges the value of the conversation and respects the views of the other.

And so, I said, as naturally as I could, "Do I know about sex?" I placed the emphasis on the personal pronoun "I" and gestured to myself as if to clarify the intent of her question, without, of course, disclosing what I knew about sex, which was, well, er uh, not something I was prepared to discuss with *her.* Not that I am uncomfortable talking about sex, mind you, but, c'mon, this woman was a complete stranger. How could she even begin a conversation in this way? The whole episode seemed surreal and bizarre.

My active listening proved even more troublesome, however. The way the words came out of my mouth, they must have sounded almost patronizing, as if I had said: "Do *I* know about sex? Well, of course, I do, honey, and I could teach you something about it, too." That was not my intent, of course, but I fear I was heard that way.

When she heard my reply, she drew back against the window wall with disgust and stared right back at me, eyes flashing, jaw set, and lips pursed to spit. "SEX?" she raised her voice as I sank into my seat as far as long legs would let me.

"Sex?" I repeated with a sheepish little-boy voice.

She roared back, "SEX?! Not SEX, SNACKS! I didn't ask you if you knew about sex, I asked you if you knew about SNACKS?!! Have they served any SNACKS on this flight, yet?!!!"

I wanted to die. Jesus, take me home. Now. Please.

"Oh, I'm so sorry. So very sorry. Yes, the beverage cart has already been down the aisle." I was slumped into my seat with my shoulders as far into the aisle as a contortionist could have taken them; the armrest separating me from the aisle pressed against my side to the point of bruising.

She glared for a moment, seeming to mutter (reasonably) under her breath: "What a weirdo." I was back in high school again, crumpled against my school locker. But I digress.

To my surprise, she leaned back toward me and held out her wrist in front of my face. Then she tapped her wrist with her fingers as she said, very slowly, syllable-by-syllable: "Do you know what T-I-M-E it is?"

I bowed my head and said, looking at my watch. "Yes, it's 2:30 P.M." She nodded and returned to her previous pose, cradled by the window. I turned the page of my *Time* magazine. We never spoke again.

When the plane landed, I promise you that 5B was off the plane so fast no one else could even see his shadow; I ran past everyone until I was safe on another concourse. I do not know what happened to the woman in 5A, but I can only imagine the story she told her family and friends.

Sex. It's a subject of universal interest and yet, a subject reluctantly approached in almost every quarter. As soon as the word appeared in the conversation on the plane, I was paralyzed. Even though she didn't ask me about sex, I thought she did, and I had no idea how to proceed. My mind was flooded with all kinds of absurd detours while she stared at me wanting to order a Diet Coke. Even with our children, our parents and, yes, our spouses, we sometimes stumble over ourselves when any serious dialog about sexuality surfaces.

And, may Heaven help us if there's a sexual conversation at church.

And yet, sex is incessantly the subject in the world around us. Over the last 30–40 years especially, sexual conversation has been mainstreamed in entertainment, in the news, in comedy, drama and everyday life.

People joke about sex. They read about sex. And, in a way, they talk about sex. *Sex and the City* is more than just the title of a television franchise; it is the emblem of a new social order. It's hard to imagine a comedy series so named on one network opposite *Ozzie and Harriet* on another in the 1960s.

This isn't necessarily bad, in my view. Sexuality should be discussed, and more openly. But how many people actually have honest and substantive conversations about sex, not masked by crude humor or demeaning stereotypes?

This brings us to our question: Why is the church averse to offering frank dialog about human sexuality along with constructive advice? Why is it that the church is the last place on the planet most people would think to turn for sexual information?

Notice how the question (which received many votes in all stages of our survey) was originally framed by its author: "Why is the church so *reluctant* to preach about strategies to avoid lust, premarital sex, and Internet pornography?" The Scriptures certainly speak about sex often.

In Paul's letters to the Corinthian Church, he speaks very plainly and, by inference, expects straightforward discussions about human sexuality to take place in the Christian community. The ancient city of Corinth was famed as a place of sweeping sexual license. Even when framed by the libertine views of human sexual conduct in the Greco-Roman world, Corinth went a step beyond. High above the city, straddling a towering acrocorinth (like the acropolis in Athens) was an opulent temple dedicated to the Greek goddess of love and sexuality, Aphrodite; the Romans called her Venus. In many readings of Greek mythology, she gave birth to Eros (or as the Romans called her son, Cupid); Eros would become the god of sexual desire. Erotic is an English word-form directly descended from the sexual template of Corinth.

The worship of Aphrodite naturally elevated fertility and human lovemaking. Temple prostitution—worship services distinguished not so much by pomp and circumstance, as by random copulation in the temple courts—became a standard fixture of Corinthian life. Temple prostitutes received offerings for their services, thought to honor the goddess, but also to profit her priests and priestesses. Becoming a female prostitute working in the temple was one of the few career paths open to women in the ancient pagan world in which they could viably achieve financial independence. It is thought that there was approximately one female prostitute in Corinth for every two men there. Up to 1,000 female prostitutes would be available at the temple each day; temple worship, as it was known, was focused on reaching men (talk about a "men's ministry"). A bell would ring throughout the city at the close of each day, calling men to worship; the men would choose the priestess/prostitute of their choice from a line-up, find their way into a chamber designed for sex, and then make an offering. It was thought that in the act of sexual intercourse, the sins of the male were transferred into the representative of the goddess.

Male priests in the service of Aphrodite also worked at the temple, although these are thought to have provided sexual favors principally for men. Homosexuality was clearly a part of the mix at the acrocorinth.

This religious and cultural frame greatly undermined values of marriage and monogamy, of course. Exclusive sexual relationships were dismissed and even discouraged. Social arrangements defining households and the raising of children adapted to this flexible order—continuing family lines by law and convention—but sexual intersections roamed routinely beyond everyone's front door. Business and pleasure seekers from around the world found their way to Corinth to worship in this way. The Corinthians, strategically managing key trade routes and hosting this extraordinary religious cult, became both fabulously wealthy and emotionally and spiritually impoverished at the same time.

It was into this world that the Apostle Paul walked. It was into this world the Church of God at Corinth was born. And it was into this world that the church spoke in a straightforward, healthy and open way about human sexuality. Paul's letters are sexually explicit; he is not reluctant to face the subject head on.

> **1 Corinthians 6:9-11**
> *"Don't you realize that those who do wrong will not inherit the Kingdom of God? Don't fool yourselves. Those who indulge in sexual sin, or who worship idols, or commit adultery, or are male prostitutes, or practice homosexuality, or are thieves, or greedy people, or drunkards, or are abusive, or cheat people—none of these will inherit the Kingdom of God. Some of you were once like that. But you were cleansed; you were made holy; you were made right with God by calling on the name of the Lord Jesus Christ and by the Spirit of our God."*

The first thing named in this catalog of caution is sexual sin. Sexual sin is then defined by illustration: certain forms of sexual conduct are explicitly listed as foreign to the Kingdom of God. Adultery. Prostitution. Homosexuality. These expressions of human sexuality are lumped together with greed, theft, drunkenness and dishonesty as unhealthy and bars to receiving God's promised Kingdom benefits.

The Bible repeatedly emphasizes that the way we manage our sexuality is of great consequence in our relationship with God. Historians suggest that the greatest distinguishing mark of the New Testament church, setting it apart from the world around it, was its sexual ethic. It was in sexual conduct that the believers found themselves most acutely at odds with cultural norms. The church could not avoid the sexual issues of its age then; it cannot now.

It does not matter how fun, how bright, how generous, how kind, how genuine, or how loving you consider yourself to be—it does not matter how much good you do or dream of doing—if your sexual conduct is outside of God's clearly expressed boundaries, your ability to enjoy God's favor and blessing is severely compromised. You will find yourself denied at the Kingdom's gate. That's the Word from Corinthians, anyway.

You may have noticed that the topic of homosexuality is addressed separately in a later chapter of this book, as one of the top ten questions in our survey focused on that area of sexuality alone. In this chapter—and addressing sexuality more broadly—know that the Bible has much to say, frankly, honestly and positively about this God-given area of life. In fact, in 2007, more than 2,000 people in Hong Kong petitioned the local government to ban the Bible because of its "sexually explicit content." The petition asked that Bibles be legal only in the possession of adults at least 18 years of age.[1]

Genesis 38:9

"But Onan was not willing to have a child who would not be his own heir. So whenever he had intercourse with his brother's wife, he spilled the semen on the ground. This prevented her from having a child who would belong to his brother."

The story of Onan illustrates the direct way in which the Scriptures record and comment on sexual conduct. Not much is left to the imagination here. We know today that Onan's method of birth control is dicey and likely to be ineffective. Nevertheless, the Bible speaks about real life situations; sexual thought and expression is a part of everyone's life. The Song of Solomon is a Bible book dedicated to whole, healthy and very sexual relationships within marriage. See how the groom in this case speaks to his bride:

> **Song of Solomon 7:6-8**
> *"Oh, how beautiful you are! How pleasing, my love, how full of delights! You are slender like a palm tree, and your breasts are like its clusters of fruit. I said, 'I will climb the palm tree and take hold of its fruit and the fragrance of your breath is like apples.'*

"I will climb the palm tree and take hold of its fruit." This phraseology is more than poetic. The Bible is not shy.

The world is speaking about sex, too. A lot.

Pornography is a $13 billion per year industry, worldwide.[2] This is money paid for the production and distribution of sexually explicit material designed to arouse. This does not refer to instructional or educationally based materials that may be necessarily graphic; this does not refer to products designed to protect sexual health and provide safety from disease; this does not include therapeutic, medical, or academic resources for the study, understanding, or treatment of human sexual health and wholeness. No, this number tallies only those sexually explicit materials offered to entertain.

Even more startling than the revenue gained each year by the sex industry is the amount of attention it receives from people across the country. Though pornographic websites account for only 1% of websites across the Internet, the traffic on those websites accounts for almost 40% of all Internet traffic.[3]

And what kinds of people are accessing these sites anyway? Isn't it just something lonely wackos do in their spare time?

Actually, 19% of Americans regularly access porn, and of that group, nearly half are married and a third have children.[4] A quarter of male college students look at porn every day or almost every day, and another quarter say they look at it once or twice a week.

And perhaps most disconcerting, in the United States today, half of all males and one-third of all females are exposed to pornography before they turn 12 years old.[5]

These are sobering figures. Many marriage and family counselors recognize now that the prevalence of and easy access to porn greatly affects both households and working environments in negative ways. At least one leading expert in the field of sexual addictions contends that online sexual activity is "a hidden public health hazard exploding, in part because very few are recognizing it as such or taking it seriously."[6]

Social boundaries defining acceptable sexual conduct have rapidly changed in the last few decades. Sexual contact between consenting adults is now the approved norm (although, in some quarters, adultery—sexual relationships involving a partner married to someone else—is still viewed negatively). The only sexual unions socially condemned in western society these days are those between adults and minors, those that are between adults, but non-consensual, and those between certain close family members. Pedophilia, rape, incest—with these three exceptions, anything goes. Welcome to Corinth.

Whatever the world around us embraces, the followers of Christ must understand the biblical mandate to travel a different path, if necessary, counter-culturally. Why then is the church silent? Why is the church reluctant to speak up in a healthy way, celebrating human sexuality by outlining boundaries for its maximum pleasure, as God designed it? Our source book speaks plainly. The secular world speaks plainly. In the marketplace of ideas, those who speak loudest and longest are heard. Why isn't the church consistently teaching, talking and openly addressing principles, strategies and healthy insights regarding our sexuality within a Christian context? Here are some ideas explaining why I believe the church has been silent:

We are fundamentally uncomfortable with our own sexuality. We do not like to look at ourselves and acknowledge that we are sexual beings, created that way by God. We have a sense of confusion about who we are. Intellectually we can argue that yes, sexuality is good, if experienced within certain boundaries. But emotionally there's something about sex that creates a block denying for some the freedom to discuss it, laugh about it, talk seriously about it or even acknowledge it. We're confused and insecure about our own sexual identities. I am not here referring to what is often termed sexual orientation; I am referring to the fundamental reality of our sexual nature, its power and presence in our lives. We don't like to think about it—or, at least, admit that we do.

Many church communities have been conditioned to believe that sexuality is inherently, subliminally, less—less-than-righteous, less-than-sacred—less than better, higher planes of human experience. Sexuality is "of the flesh" and that somehow makes it stained.

Think about our vocabulary, the way we use the English language to talk about sex. If I were to say that I just heard a "dirty" story, what kind of story would I be talking about? How would you interpret that? You would think I was describing a story that had sexual content. If I were to tell you that someone was talking to me and made an "off-color" remark, what would you think I was describing? Not a remark about the colors of the rainbow or ethnicity—you would know it was about some sort of sexual innuendo, reference or bald comment. Dirty. Off-color. Sex. All cut from the same cloth.

Our language is framed to reflect our worldview, which in this case, is that sex is, well, dirty. It's base. It needs to be kept under wraps, out of view. It must never be introduced into polite conversation at mealtimes or at church. Like cockroaches, sewers, and other unfortunate realities, we speak in hushed tones about things we know exist but want to keep in the shadows.

We're afraid of its power. Instinctively, we know that if we play with fire it might burn the house down. With fire, it is better not to even touch the matches or talk about doing so, because then the prospects can become too dangerous, too real. We know that sex has power, and because we know it does, it seems safer to run away from it than to face it and take the chance it might consume us.

Its power is intense, and it can overwhelm. These are truths, after all. But those truths should not discourage us from harnessing the power and energy of fire. Or sex.

Instead of learning how to celebrate and manage the flame, we are prone to focus instead on the damage it has done. Human sexuality has been the source of much abuse and wrongdoing, no doubt about it. Like anything that has great capacity for good, our sexuality has great capacity for evil. It can blind us to the right, breed selfishness, prompt impulsive and destructive behaviors and cause otherwise thoughtful men and women to see one another as objects and playthings.

Consequently, we've too often dismissed our sexuality as a function of our lower nature, competing with, instead of complementing, God's light in our lives.

We fear rejection. If we talk about sexuality and how important we personally consider it to be, we fear social ostracism or rejection. Never mind that our sexuality is at the core of our being.

Social rejection can happen in all sorts of places, in all kinds of ways. It is always painful. You might be rejected from a starting role on the football team. You might be pulled from the basketball court in the last minutes of a close game because your coach doesn't trust your ability to deliver under pressure. You could be removed from the program because you are not considered skilled enough at the piano to be included in the recital. Your painting does not make the cut for the school's art exhibition. Erica says, "No, thank you," when you ask her to go out with you on Friday night. You lose the Student Council election; your peers vote in larger numbers for someone else than they do for you. Ouch. These are all difficult moments to endure, but, for the most part, we do endure and move on, in the end.

But as we grow and mature, none of us wants to face rejection based on our sexual perspectives, questions or desire, because these go to the core of who we are. I may never be the key to the ballgame, master the piano or win an election; my reputation can remain intact even if I take some risks in these areas. But I will not risk my social standing because I spoke about sexuality in a way that might raise anyone's eyebrows. It's too incendiary. What will others think about me? Sexual conversation is off limits, especially at church. It's safer that way.

Every couple I counsel before marriage is required to talk about each partner's sexuality before marriage; each partner is required to discuss their sexual histories, hopes and fears. As I deliver the assignment across my desk, there is often nervous laughter, a glance out the window or at the floor, an awkward pause. Again, many people are accustomed to talking about sex at a superficial level, even joking about it, but few are comfortable actually discussing honestly and authentically what they harbor inside. Many married people never speak about it. They avoid in-depth conversation, moving to other things. Anyone can have a sexual relationship without talking, of course, but no one can develop a growing sense of intimacy and keep their sexuality fresh and alive in silence.

Why are even husbands and wives reluctant to talk seriously about sex? It's all about the fear of rejection.

For instance, if I told my wife that there were certain sexual activities that make me feel uncomfortable and are, consequently, off limits in our relationship, she might reject me. I'm not suggesting she'd leave me for another man, but she might become frustrated and reply, "What? Did I marry some kind of prude? Did you grow up in a cave? Isn't this the 21st century? C'mon. Grow up." My wife wouldn't speak to me in this way (and, truth be told, I can't imagine any sexual activity in my marriage that doesn't appeal to me), but I have heard some wives speak in this way. It is worse than withering. It is humiliating. Better to be silent and keep my sexual hang-ups to myself.

What if I explained to her that I really wanted to try something different in our marriage bed, experimenting in territory previously unexplored. She might pull back in disgust, responding to my honest approach by saying, "You monster. Creep! I can't believe you would even think of such a thing. How did I get stuck with a sicko like you?" Again, my wife would never push me away so cruelly. In either of these scenarios, great risks are assumed. Crushing consequences could result. Silence is safety. We repress our sexual interest, feed resentments in the hidden closets of our heart, juggle frustrations and play it safe, fearing open conversation about our sexuality, even in our bedrooms.

So we don't talk about sex constructively at all at home. It's no wonder, then, that we don't talk about sex at church, either.

I've experienced my moments of fear at church, afraid that introducing sexual content into a sermon might compromise my standing. In the 1990s, I began the custom of addressing human sexuality from the Sunday pulpit at least once every year. It's the annual "Sex Talk." In the eyes of some, I've consequently devolved into a kind of talk-about-sex-all-the-time-from-the-pulpit pastor. It's an absurd charge, but it demonstrates how uncomfortable people can be with the subject on Sunday, even if just once a year.

Last year, working together with a local Christian psychologist, two Christian physicians, and a Christian mental health professional specializing in male sexuality, I introduced a Survey of Male Sexuality. The survey was distributed throughout our congregation and through other churches in our community, as well. It asked respondents explicit questions about their sexuality, covering everything from masturbation to prostitution to the age of first sexual experience and so on. The results produced a fascinating snapshot of what men in our community—not in New York or Denver or San Francisco—were thinking, doing and contemplating.

As we tabulated the survey results, our church learned how to best tune its ministry to men to call the best out of them, empower them to manage their sexuality appropriately and encourage them to embrace their God-given masculinity. The survey results were first released at a Men's Retreat, in which the guys were invited to ask anything about sexuality, the Bible, God's parameters and more. What a rich and productive exercise in relevant ministry it proved to be!

But, some of the criticism we received for even conceiving the survey, let alone distributing it, was scathing. By far, the most slicing critiques came from folks in other churches, fuming at the "shameful" and "degenerate" nature of the whole enterprise. "How could you possibly think Jesus would be honored by such a thing?" one correspondent railed, "I am appalled you think yourself a preacher of the Gospel."

Why don't we talk about sex in church? That's why. People in the church reject those who talk about it. But I cannot reconcile that rejection with the God I know and the God revealed in the Scriptures.

Surely God would not give us a gift for which He did not have a whole and pure purpose. God would not have created Adam and Eve, set them in the Garden naked, and walked with them in the cool of the evening and said, "It is good," if it was not.

Surely He would not have commanded that "the two shall become one," inviting them to a marriage bed, if the very act of marriage itself (a sexual union) was to be ever after considered shameful and somehow anti-spiritual. Our sexuality is not antithetical to our walk with God, and it does not, in and of itself, push us away from Him.

1 Corinthians 6:13-20
"But you can't say that our bodies were made for sexual immorality. They were made for the Lord, and the Lord cares about our bodies. And God will raise us from the dead by his power, just as he raised our Lord from the dead.

Don't you realize that your bodies are actually parts of Christ? Should a man take his body, which is part of Christ, and join it to a prostitute? Never! And don't you realize that if a man joins himself to a prostitute, he becomes one body with her? For the Scriptures say, "The two are united into one." But the person who is joined to the Lord is one spirit with him.

> *Run from sexual sin! No other sin so clearly affects the body as this one does. For sexual immorality is a sin against your own body. Don't you realize that your body is the temple of the Holy Spirit, who lives in you and was given to you by God? You do not belong to yourself, for God bought you with a high price. So you must honor God with your body."*

It's a tall order. A sacred teaching. It's an open door for us to talk in an open way about strategies to manage our sexuality. Here are some strategies I believe can be substantiated in Scripture—strategies to help you embrace and manage your sexuality in a whole and healthy way:

First, acknowledge yourself as a sexual being. Stop trying to pretend otherwise. Don't run away from it. Don't try to repress or deny it. And do not be ashamed by the fact that you are interested in sex, that you're curious about sex, that you like sex and that your sexuality is a God-given gift. Stop allowing the enemy of your soul to clothe you with guilt because you sometimes think about sex. Stop trying to ignore the reality that God wired you this way, and you are a sexual being. Stop punishing yourself because your body responds to certain stimuli. Stop trying to be asexual. You were not created to be a eunuch.

God created us, male or female, powerfully wired with a sexual interest. You have a sexual appetite that is a gift from God. Own it. Celebrate it. How you manage it is the next step. But first, you must acknowledge the gift and thank God for it.

Repression of your sexuality can only make it more likely that the devil will use it against you. God cannot redeem what you do not surrender; you cannot surrender what you do not acknowledge. You cannot acknowledge what you pretend does not exist.

This gift of sex was not given only for the propagation of the human race, either. While procreation can be a very important—and sacred—outcome of a sexual relationship, it is not the single object of our sexuality. Even if you never conceive a child, God is pleased for you to enjoy His gift of sex. Pleasure is as much a part of the gift as is procreation.

My mother makes the finest lemon meringue pie in the world; that's my view, anyway. She has, for as long as I can remember, made a lemon meringue pie that's a little different from most others. I like lemon meringue pie in all of its forms; most often it has a gelatin-like lemon filling under the meringue. But my mother's lemon meringue is more of a cream pie. The meringue is always perfectly wafted across the lemon filling—a filling so tart and sweet as to leave my head spinning. Sweet and sour, creamy and dreamy. I have no idea how many cups of sugar must go into the filling or how much lemon juice is used, but I know that with every bite my taste buds will be rushed with pain and pleasure. Yes, it's kind of a sensual treat. I like it. A lot.

Even now as an adult, my mother will sometimes make that lemon meringue pie for me. Yes, me, her son. She does not make it to taunt or tease me. She does not bake the pie so that I can look longingly at it on the counter. She does not create it just to nourish my body with egg protein in the meringue and vitamin C in the lemon juice. She bakes that pie and gives it to me because it tastes good, and she knows I will enjoy it. It's a treat, a pleasure to consume. She wants me to enjoy it, because she's my mom and she loves me. It's a gift. Enjoy.

God's gift of sex is given in the same way. He gave it to you to enjoy. It does not have to have any other purpose. Own that about yourself. The God that bestowed this gift in Eden's perfect day, the God that inspired the Song of Solomon, the God that encouraged Corinthian husbands and wives to give their spouses the gift of sex, the God that extols the wonder of "two becoming one flesh," is the God who made you a sexual being. Enjoy.

Second, establish sexual boundaries. Without boundaries, your sexuality will destroy you; the devil will use it to destroy you (and others you touch, as well). You must decide what your boundaries will be. Where will you draw the lines? Let the Bible be your guide.

I believe the most important biblical sexual boundaries can be summarized in this way:

Sexual expression that involves your genitals, in the company of another person, is forbidden unless that person is your spouse. In the company of your spouse, you are free to express yourself sexually in any way that is consensual and exclusively honors and respects your spouse.

Or, in other words, shared sexual experience must be reserved for marriage; within marriage there is broad freedom to explore and enjoy.

If you are reading this book and are currently in a relationship that involves sexual expression with someone who is not your spouse, stop it today. Not tomorrow. Today. Today is the day. It will not be easier later. It will not make more sense later. Postponing this ultimate commitment to biblical sexuality will make things worse and more difficult. You cannot love someone else, honor someone else or respect someone else by enabling them to do wrong. By the measure of God's Word, shared sexuality outside of marriage is wrong. It's as simple, as challenging, as counter-cultural as that.

Continuing in a sexual relationship outside of marriage cannot bless you or your partner; it cannot enhance your relationship with God. It can only undermine your spiritual health, drive a wedge between you and the Lord and act as a block when you approach Heaven in prayer.

Sex outside of marriage compromises every aspect of your relationship with God, including your ability to be heard in prayer. This is not because God is punitive and pouts, but because our sin always creates a barrier. Remember, in the first Corinthian letter, Paul warns us that sexual sin is like no other; it is a sin against our own bodies, bodies purchased with a high price, the price of Jesus' own blood. We must honor God with our bodies. Sexual sin demeans them. Let it go. Start fresh and let God, in time, show you how to experience your sexuality in a guilt-free and holistic way.

You have to know where your boundaries are, and you have to stick to them.

There's another boundary that might be called a demilitarized zone. Identify your limits and then create a margin—a line drawn a little farther in, so that you are not required to fight temptations hard and fast against your core commitments. A margin—a demilitarized zone—can help protect you from a fateful slip. Don't park your car in front of the Baskin-Robins store if you do not want to buy ice cream. Don't place yourself in situations where you know the sexual tension will be tough to resist.

It's best to set your boundaries when the pressure is off, not in the middle of a heated battle with your senses. Don't wait until you're in a crisis to sort your boundaries out.

Third, find an accountability partner. How do I know where exactly to set my boundaries, beyond the fundamental propositions outlined above? That's a question that could be addressed in another book entirely. But here's a good place to start: establish a relationship with another person of the same gender who can hold you accountable. This accountability partner should be someone you trust and respect, someone who has the capacity to stare you down at regular intervals on your calendar and ask you tough questions about your sexual conduct and someone with wisdom to help you sort out specific boundaries and apply them to the unique circumstances of your life. The devil will challenge every biblically framed sexual boundary you purpose to observe, I promise; find an accountability partner who will challenge you from the right side of the line as well.

Every pastor on our local church staff is required to have a person like that in their life, myself included. I meet with my accountability partner routinely and review the weaknesses, the Achilles' heals, in my life. We review how I manage my sexuality. I'm a regular guy, like everybody else, and when I sit down with my accountability partner I walk through where I've been, what I've been thinking, where my danger zones are and so on. I have to stay clean in between our visits or be prepared to admit failure or lie. It's a lot easier to stay clean.

All of us need someone like that in our lives. Even with such an arrangement, living within God's parameters sexually can be a daunting challenge. But it can be done—and it always pays rich dividends when we do so.

Fourth, make sure that the topic of sexuality is on the table at your house and in your church in a healthy way. Sexual conversation in your home should not be something only whispered, kept as a secret. Referencing our sexuality should not be removed from all ordinary dialogue. Relegating sexuality to the shadows and edges of the room only reinforces the false notion that this sacred gift is really soiled in some way.

There is a time and place for everything, of course. Sexual subjects are not always appropriate anytime, anywhere. Children should not be exposed to concepts that they are too young to comprehend; husbands and wives must honor each other by reserving intimate details for their bedroom alone. But the occasional reference to the differences between men and women, the need for dad and mom to cuddle alone together, the sacredness of the marriage bed, the wonder of conception and human life, the beauty of romance, and more, should be welcomed and introduced along the way.

Speak to your pastor if your church does not speak of human sexuality. Speak up for age-level appropriate curriculum about God's design for sexuality in your child and student ministries; lay foundations today that can lead to healthy sexual boundaries later. Never imagine that most children and teens receive healthy instruction at home. It is far more likely that many young people in your church are introduced to their sexuality by porn discovered on the Internet.

Encourage conferences, seminars and question-and-answer sessions for adults throughout the year in which open and honest conversation about sexuality can be heard and, yes, enjoyed, in your church. Help people in your church feel safe to speak of such things; foster the idea that when people have questions about their sexuality, church should be the first place they go to seek answers, not the last.

We would like to think our children are insulated from the Corinthian culture around us. But even when the television and computer are carefully screened at home, we cannot control exposure in other people's homes or on a friend's cell phone. We must be proactive, intentional and brave: make sexual conversation a natural and balanced part of your home and church life.

Studies show that children between the ages of eight and nine are at an intellectual threshold where they are most amenable to understanding and adopting their parents' sexual values. Most of us do not speak with our children about sexual themes until much later, rendering much of what we consider "sex ed" to be too late. By the time our children reach adolescence, they have already shaped and formed large parts of their sexual identities and value sets. Remember, the average child in the United States will view pornographic material by age twelve.

If you have not been alongside to help steer the course before puberty, your children will have a hard time developing into whole, sexual adults. And if you think you can wait until your children are fifteen or sixteen, when you are also expressing concern about their hair, their driving, their curfews, their music, their friends and more, it's going to be very difficult to persuade them to tune in for your sexuality course.

At every age, emphasize the positive, not the negative. Be the person who can laugh about sex. Be the person who can talk about sex. Be the person who does not blanche when sex suddenly appears in a conversation (as I did on the plane to Charlotte).

If someone makes an inappropriate reference, speak up and make it clear the remark was out of bounds. But if someone simply speaks honestly and respectfully, speak up and let them know you are someone with whom they can feel safe to talk.

And, fifth, protect yourself on the Internet. Secure a filter for home, for work, for your laptop, if necessary. There are many software programs that can do the job; some will allow you to link with an accountability partner, providing another level of safety. Place your computer in a place where the screen can be seen by others. If you find yourself wandering on the Web into places you shouldn't go, 'fess up. Disclose.

Internet porn can be intoxicating. Hours can be wasted. Dollars can be squandered. Minds can be bent. Once tasted, it can be tough to disengage. Again, find an accountability partner to help. You are not alone. Don't try to act alone.

Sexuality is fundamental to who we are. It is a dimension of human experience that we should celebrate. God wrote the definitive book on the subject; let's study, discuss, and learn from it.

I cannot know where you've been in life, sexually. Maybe you've been wounded or abused. Maybe you have wounded or abused someone else. Maybe you have stepped outside of God's boundaries. Maybe you have lived within them.

Wherever you have been, be encouraged. God has the power—and He has the will—to redeem, to polish and to bless your sexuality, if you make the choice to honor Him with it. Hear, once more, the Word given to the Corinthian believers, as it is to us: "Some of you were once like that. But you were cleansed; you were made holy; you were made right with God by calling on the name of the Lord Jesus Christ and by the Spirit of our God."

Some of the members of the Corinthian church—perhaps most of them—were shadowed by their sexual past. But they were made clean, they were made holy, just the same by calling on the name of Jesus. The same can be said for us, if we are willing to call on the Name.

Why is the church so reluctant to talk about sex and its challenges? We're insecure and afraid. We fear its power. We fear rejection.

In the church where I pastor, sex is recognized as a good, holy and positive thing. We own it. We acknowledge it. We talk about it. You can, too.

Question 7

Death and What's Next

"What happens when we die in Christ? Do we go straight to Heaven or do we wait in the ground? Or what?"

Most of us rarely deal with death. Death takes center stage, of course, when it occasionally comes close. When one deeply loved passes away, we may find ourselves staring at an empty chair, wondering how we can move forward with life, struggling with a loss from which there seems no escape. The passing of a family member or a friend? We can be left paralyzed, spent and confused. Even the passing of someone we do not know but whose end we witness in a tragic turn of events can cast a long shadow in our otherwise ordered lives. A health scare in our own journey—a doctor's diagnosis or life-threatening injury—this, too, can take our breath away. All of these brushes with mortality, though, are relatively rare. We're able to ignore death most of the time, and we're glad to do so. We try not to think about it. It's too dark. Too difficult. Too painful. Too mysterious. Too, well, too beyond our ability to control.

Some of us, on the other hand, are required to deal with death routinely. It is not uncommon for me, as a pastor, to be called to the bedside of someone who is passing from this world to the next or to officiate at a funeral for a member of my church family. More often than you would imagine, pastors are also called to officiate at funeral services for people they do not know and may have never met; you might be surprised by how many people there are in this world who have no one else to speak for them.

Facing death is always sobering. It can be painful for those left behind; it can be accompanied by a kind of despair and helplessness that defy language—a kind of ache deep down inside that cannot be spoken, for which words fail. Still, death must be faced. It is one of the few inevitables in life, one of the few threads woven into every life, a bookend shared by all of us, without regard to our origins, beliefs or preferences.

We're all going to die. I am going to die. You are going to die. The question, of course, for each of us is not "if" but "when?" There is coming a day when the hands with which you hold this book, the eyes with which you read this book, and the brain with which you digest this book will all lie lifeless, useless, dead. Your body will no longer be animate; it will be vacant, empty, cold. And what happens then? Once the physical frame I so naturally describe as "myself" is stilled, am I also ended? Or are our bodies, in fact, not "ourselves?" Are our bodies simply residences, occupied for a time, and then abandoned? And, if we are more than our bodies, what then? Where do we go from here? That is the question of the ages. It is *the* matter of life and death.

Death is a most interesting subject: the most absolute and universally accepted reality is also the one we prefer most often to avoid. Strange, really. Yet understandable at the same time: we are prone to fear the unknown and those intersections in life from which we know there can be no return, whatever the outcome.

The Scriptures are not squeamish on this count, though. They speak freely and naturally about death and what happens to us as we walk through that extraordinary doorway. The Bible is especially direct, as it speaks to people of faith, who (as the Apostle Paul likes to put it in his letters to the New Testament churches) die "in Christ."

As with other questions posed and addressed in this book, the tough subjects with which we wrestle in life—and the tough questions that so easily take us to the mat—are consistently, clearly and definitively answered in the Bible with brilliant lines of truth and reason drawn throughout the Old and New Testament narratives.

What happens when we die in Christ? Start staring down death here:

Hebrews 9:27-28

"And just as each person is destined to die once and after that comes judgment, so also Christ died once for all time as a sacrifice to take away the sins of many people."

The jury is still out in the debate about who was the human instrument God used to give us the book of Hebrews; traditionally, the Apostle Paul has been thought to be the author, although there are those who think otherwise (and with plausible reason). Whoever penned the lines above, the Holy Spirit inspired them, and they first emphasize the truth we have already claimed: we are all going to die. You may not get the doctor's appointment for which you hoped, or the job appointment for which you have strived, or the academic appointment of which you've dreamed, but there's one appointment on your calendar, that, like it or not, you will meet: you have an appointment to die. Yes, you.

The first step in answering the question—and dealing with the subject—is to come to terms with your own mortality. Make it personal. We are not talking about someone else's passing here. We are not talking about your friend or your loved one. We are talking about you. What will happen to you when you die? Because you will. The only part of the mortality equation that is uncertain is the timing. Today? Tomorrow? Fifty years from now? You do not know. Heaven knows. Time will tell. The appointment is on the books. It's going to happen. *Ouch.*

There's an online calculator that synthesizes public health statistics from around the world to estimate the number of people at death's door at any given moment. So far today—the day on which I am writing this chapter for this book—52,110 people have died.[1] And, I mean just *so far.* I'm writing at 8:00 A.M. and more than 52,000 people have died since the clock turned from one day to the next, worldwide (not counting political upheavals and acts of war). In a way, it's a crude estimate, of course—no one can know exactly how many people have passed away in any given minute. But, the guestimate can come close. The data is strong.

If you're reading right now after 8:00 A.M., it is safe to say that more than 52,000 have left their bodies behind already since this new day began. If we multiply that number by three (52,000 people passing away every eight hours—there are three eight hour segments every 24-hour day), 156,000 will be gone before midnight.

By mid-year, more than 28,000,000 will be gone. And the number of deaths grows exponentially every year, as the world's population expands. The number is never stagnant. Where have all those people gone? Did they go anywhere? Someday, each of us will also be a part of that number.

Will it be an accident? A heart attack? Cancer? A drunk driver? Pneumonia? Falling asleep behind the wheel? What will be the circumstance of our own passing? We cannot know. We just know there will be one.

I am convinced that no one is ever really free to live until he faces his own death; none of us can experience wholeness in this life while pretending we can continually postpone considering the consequences of our own death. Coming to terms with the reality of your death is the first step to coming to terms with the potential of your life.

The Hebrews passage does more than just acknowledge the inevitability of death, however. It also declares what happens next: "then will come the judgment."

Our ability to influence our future disposition—that is, where we find ourselves for eternity—ends when our life on earth ends. There is not an intermediate waiting room in which you can sort things out for a better final outcome after you leave your body behind. Those you leave behind will not be able to alter your course once the hands with which you hold this book drop lifeless. The dye will then already have been cast, by your choices and no one else's. Purgatory or any equivalent is not a place or a concept with much traction in Scripture.

What happens when I die? My eternal destiny is sealed at the moment of my passing. There is not a second act after I die with a stage onto which I might walk and try to deliver my lines better. Once the curtain drops, the show is over. You have an appointment to die. And then comes the judgment.

If you carry unresolved guilt and shame in this life, then you will carry it across the threshold of the grave and to the judgment seat. If you cling to baggage stuffed with your failures, regrets and resentments today in this world, then you will not be able to let go of that baggage as you enter the world to come, either. If you do not, in this life, make peace with God and find a way to wash your dirty clothes here below, then you will wear them stained, standing in the courtroom of eternity above and be condemned. It's that simple.

All of us have sinned, all of us have messed up. All of us have failed. All of us have been less than our best. All of us have betrayed, by our thoughts and conduct, the perfect call of our Maker. Never allow yourself to imagine that you will get a pass at Heaven's gate because, although not perfect you are somehow not so bad—especially when measured by some of the other bad guys who have walked through this world. The judgment's plumbline will not be the conduct of others, but the model of Christ and the law of God. Unless we have lived to perfection, without flaw, we are doomed.

The Gospel of Christ, however, is focused on exactly this dilemma. How can we pass through the judgment unscathed and be welcomed by a holy God? How can we, soiled and stained as we are, find our place on Heaven's cul-de-sac and not be left, instead, on the devil's curb and in his company forever? The work (and *work* seems like an altogether inadequate term to fully describe what He has done) of Jesus on the Cross has made a way for us to be free from shame and guilt, to unload the heavy baggage of our failures and petty grudges and to wash our clothes clean, so that once we die and face the judgment, we do so with confidence, bathed by grace. Covered by Christ, with Christ as our Advocate at the bench and with the promise of God's favor in Christ, we can die and move through the judgment without fear.

But we must humble ourselves and embrace this free gift of life in this world before we move forward to the next. The gift is on the table here, not there. Anglo-Saxon law (which is the legal platform in American jurisprudence as it is elsewhere in the English-speaking world) has a maxim: a gift is not a gift until it is received. A gift promised to you is not recognized as yours, by law, until you receive it. If I decline a gift today, then I cannot later demand that it be offered to me again tomorrow. I have no legal rights to possess the gift until I receive it. The gift of eternal life in Christ is offered today. Do not trifle with it. It may not be there for you tomorrow, because we all have an appointment to die.

But wait. Isn't all of this just nonsense? Are any of us really going to live on after our bodies give out and we die? Isn't it just wishful thinking? Maybe my body is myself, after all; perhaps, I am nothing more than a finely evolved physical expression of blind natural forces in a material universe—a chemically-induced mirage of consciousness and meaning.

Let's visit Job, once more. Job is famous for suffering unjustly. His journey through life was a series of catastrophic, crushing losses. He lost his family, his wealth, his health. The only thing that still remained in his possession at the end of the day was an almost-extinguished, fragile, invisible thread of life. As Job struggled with the proposition of surviving in the wake of unspeakable pain, he posed this question:

> **Job 14:14**
> *"Can the dead live again? If so, this would give me hope through all my years of struggle, and I would eagerly await the release of death."*

Life in this world is hard, and hard to bear. Is it possible that my life has potential beyond this broken world? Can I live again, beyond and better? Is it possible that my life could be reconstituted in such a way that I could be free of sorrow and empowered to enjoy, be blessed and not fear? Is there hope of a world to come in which the mud and sludge of today's pathways are forgotten as we tread streets of gold? If so, I can keep moving forward, no matter how difficult the road, knowing there are better days ahead. If I know my great expectations are to be realized, I can endure the challenges of the present hour. And so Job asked the question: Is it possible that I could live again after I die?

The question asked in the Old Testament by Job is answered in the New Testament by Paul. Will we live again?

> **2 Corinthians 5:8**
> *"Yes, we are fully confident, and we would rather be away from these earthly bodies, for then we will be at home with the Lord."*

Job and Paul shared much in common: both endured extraordinary hardships. Like Job, Paul was no stranger to suffering. His life was blanketed with physical pain, social ostracism, outrageous slander and prejudice, material deprivation, exhausting crises, beatings, shackles and worse. Yet he says that when our *persona*—the core of who we are, the true spirit and soul of self—is separated from the body into which we were first born, then we are, quite literally, with the Lord. We are not dead. We are not zeroes. We do not disappear into nothing, vanished and vanquished.

You will die; your eternal destination and relationship to God is determined before you die; if you die in Christ you will find yourself straightway with Him.

Paul has more to say along this line:

Philippians 1:21
"For to me, living means living for Christ, and dying is even better."

Because when I die, I see Him more clearly, with greater understanding—and I am released from the vulnerabilities and challenges of this world.

1 Corinthians 13:12
"Now we see things imperfectly as in a cloudy mirror, but then we will see everything with perfect clarity. All that I know now is partial and incomplete, but then I will know everything completely, just as God now knows me completely."

Clarity. A world of confusion left behind for a world of understanding and peace. Complete comprehension. All of the pieces of the puzzle perfectly fit into place. Wholeness. Holiness. All of this is contained in a conscious, tangible, electrifying passage of a lifetime from life through death to life again. When you die in Christ, you die into the Presence of Jesus.

If this is true, when does it happen? Is there a gap in time between my death and my face-to-face meeting with the Lord? Will I wait in line? In the ground? In some unknown in-between?

No. See how the process is disclosed in the crucifixion narrative in Luke's Gospel. As Jesus hangs, near death, on the Cross, two others share his fate, one on either side. There are three crosses that day on Golgotha's hill. One of the men crucified with Christ has no regrets; he owns no responsibility for his fate; he curses God and everyone else around him. Even fast approaching death's door, he is bitter and mean-spirited, perverse. He spits at Jesus, insulting and demeaning Him. His future is being sealed in those moments—this thief on his own cross is, by his own heart and hand, doomed forever.

The other man experiences the same pain and agony, but reacts quite differently. He owns his stuff, acknowledging his guilt before both God and men. He takes responsibility for the failures that have nailed him to a tree, and he speaks humbly to Jesus.

Luke 23:42-43
"Then he said, 'Jesus, remember me when you come into your Kingdom.' And Jesus replied, 'I assure you, today you will be with me in paradise.'"

This companion in death believes in the singular goodness and power of Christ. How or why he knows Jesus has supernatural power and wields it with grace is not clear, but that he knows it is very clear. He professes his faith in Christ out loud and hopes that the Lord will tenderly hear his cry. By all accounts a criminal convicted of a capital offense, he nevertheless dares to ask Jesus for mercy. He acknowledges he has lived wretchedly; he acknowledges that he is powerless to alter his deserved punishment; he acknowledges Jesus as Lord; he acknowledges that only Jesus can save him now.

This scene captures the whole plan of salvation. This is how all of us must receive the gift of life, reconciling ourselves, broken and hopeless, with God in Christ.

How does Jesus reply? He will reply to us in the same way as He did to that man when our time to die looms large: "Today you will be with me in paradise."

Not next week. Not after I return. Not after I crush the devil and his minions at the last. Not after your relatives have a chance to try and clean up your mess. Not after anything else. No. Today. Today you will be with Me in paradise. Now. You will be in a place prepared before the foundation of the world for those who love God. Surrounded by life and goodness. You will be with Me in the house of the Lord forever. You will dwell with Me. I'm not sending you on ahead of Me and you're not waiting around here for Me, either. You, Mr. Thief-on-a-cross, are going with Me, Jesus-Son-of-God, to paradise. Right away.

That's the Lord's word to all of us who honor Him.

You will die; before you die, you will determine what happens next; if you die in Christ, you will immediately to be with Him.

If that's what happens, though, what about the idea of "sleeping?" People often talk about "falling asleep" in Christ. It is a New Testament vocabulary, after all. Perhaps you have heard something like this said at a funeral or graveside service: "May he rest in peace."

Revelation 14:13
"And I heard a voice from heaven saying, 'Write this down: Blessed are those who die in the Lord from now on. Yes, says the Spirit, they are blessed indeed, for they will rest from their hard work; for their good deeds follow them!'"

In this passage, we find a euphemism—a metaphor—for death called sleep. It is found elsewhere in the Scriptures, too. Examine the story of Lazarus, for instance. Lazarus is a friend of Jesus who falls gravely ill and ultimately dies. The sisters of Lazarus send for Jesus before their brother dies, hoping He will arrive in time to heal him. Jesus arrives after the passing of Lazarus, however. In the text below, we hear the Lord explaining to the sisters of Lazarus that they should be hopeful and not distraught as He prepares to bring life back into the dead man's body. The raising of Lazarus from the dead sets the stage for the Lord's own Passion Week, which will shortly follow.

John 11:11-13
"Then he said, 'Our friend Lazarus has fallen asleep, but now I will go and wake him up.' The disciples said, 'Lord, if he is sleeping, he will soon get better!' They thought Jesus meant Lazarus was simply sleeping, but Jesus meant Lazarus had died."

Jesus described death as sleep. How can Jesus say on one hand: "Today you will be with me in paradise," as I'm dying, and, on another hand, describe my death as equivalent to sleep? Am I destined to rest in Heaven's hotel, passed out on a bed (albeit a comfortable one, no doubt) until Jesus wakes me up?

The metaphor of sleep is intertwined with the idea that we are not our bodies—that our bodies are transient residences that house us for a season, but not the sum of who we are. As already mentioned, you are not your body.

We often refer to ourselves as our bodies. How would I describe myself? I might answer the question this way: I am male, six feet, two inches tall, 185 pounds, blue eyes, with light brown hair. This would be an altogether reasonable and accurate response. But is that physical description really who I am? Would another approach to the question be more accurate?

How would I describe myself? I am a guy wrestling with the questions of life, devoted to my family and faith, trying to negotiate my way through this world without causing harm and even hoping to leave it a bit better than when I found it. I am sometimes afraid, sometimes confident and sometimes uncertain. I love to laugh and tell stories and am trying to learn to listen more. I believe God created me and loves me—even though I do not deserve His love. I believe Jesus is Lord.

Whatever the condition of my body, the last paragraph will be true. I am, most accurately, not defined by the color of my eyes or my height. I am best described by the qualities of life and thought that inhabit my body and employ it as an instrument of my true self.

Much grief can be experienced when we limit the definition of ourselves—and others—to a physical description. When we do so, we deny the reality that we are created in the image of God, an image not born in our physique so much as in our ability to create, to love and to be loved. We alone in all of the creation have been given an eternal soul. Created in the image of God, He has designed the body to house our soul; the house is not who we are.

Interestingly, when Jesus was resurrected from the dead, He was not recognized when people saw His body. He was recognized by the sound of His voice—and then sometimes only after long conversations in which He expressed His thoughts and Spirit. Mary Magdalene at the Garden Tomb, the two disciples on the road to Emmaus: it was not the physical presence of the resurrected Christ that was first understood, it was the disclosure of His inner self. There was something in the way in which He projected His Spirit by speaking—even just the speaking of Mary's name, for instance—that triggered recognition. He was not His body, He was more than that. And so will we be; and so we are.

When Jesus said Lazarus had fallen asleep, I believe He was referring to the way in which his physical body had fallen asleep. Paul said that the bodies of God's people who pass away before Jesus returns a second time had fallen asleep and would be awakened. We know in the story of Lazarus that Jesus went to the tomb, spoke to Lazarus and supernaturally reunited the spirit of Lazarus with his body. The body of Lazarus then stood tall once again, reanimated, awakened. Only his body was asleep.

When we properly speak of God's people falling asleep in death, we speak of the sleep of their bodies, not their souls.

When I officiate at graveside services, I often refer to my own journey in this world, explaining that I grew up in Seattle and moved to Indiana only later as I approached forty years of age. I describe my family's annual pilgrimage from central Indiana to the hallowed shores of Puget Sound every summer since then, as we reunite with family and friends there. And, with every trip "home" to Seattle, I take a few minutes to drive past the house in which I grew up.

I turn right off a winding arterial to climb a steep hill before turning right again on the street I used to call home. It slices along the side of the hill, with houses above the street on one side and below the street on the other. At last, the street bends downward, still hugging the hillside and ends abruptly, with no outlet, bordered by three houses. One of those is, well was, mine.

A beautiful wooded ravine surrounded the end of the street (and our house) when I was a child growing up there; it still does. How I loved to play in those woods!

The same builder constructed all three of the houses on the dead end, edging the wooded ravine; ours was finished in 1965; my parents bought it brand-new, landscaping outside and customizing finishing touches inside. As my car heads over the crest of the street, approaching the cul-de-sac, my heart begins to pound faster. My old phone number comes to mind. My head is rushed with memories—everything from playing with my toy car collection on the dirt bank out back to the day I sat behind the wheel of my first car at age 16, in the driveway, and so on. But, inevitably, I also grow frustrated as I pull up in front.

My wife always tries to discourage me from making this trip down memory lane; she knows how troubled I become every time. My parents sold the house 35 years ago. The subsequent owners have not maintained it in the way to which I was accustomed. What happened to the beautiful dogwood tree my dad planted out front? Where are the geraniums that lined the kitchen walk? What were they thinking when they painted it that hideous color? Did they actually cut into the clean roofline for that goofy greenhouse-skylight? I just don't get it.

"Jim," my wife tugs on my arm, gently. "Don't be so upset. You don't live here anymore. Treasure the memory, but let go. *It's not your house anymore.*"

It is the house in which I once lived, but no more. When you stand at a graveside and see a body lowered, it is important to realize that it is now an old address; treasure the memory, but make no mistake about it, no one lives there anymore. We all leave our old addresses—our bodies—behind.

There are actually two biblical characters named Lazarus: one the friend of Jesus, raised from the dead; the other a poor man, begging for food to survive. This second, impoverished Lazarus takes center stage in a story Jesus told. It is not clear from the context whether Jesus was describing an historic figure named Lazarus or illustrating an important truth with a parable, fictionally bringing the idea to life. Generally, Jesus introduced His parables with a qualifier like, "the Kingdom of God is like this," or "let me tell you a story." The story of poor Lazarus is not prefaced in this way; it's presented almost as if it were history. Some have speculated that this second Lazarus may also have been a friend of Jesus and that Jesus simply related the experience of His friend. In any case, the story of this Lazarus captures and communicates important truths.

Luke 16:19-23a
"Jesus said, 'There was a certain rich man who was splendidly clothed in purple and fine linen and who lived each day in luxury. At his gate lay a poor man named Lazarus who was covered with sores. As Lazarus lay there longing for scraps from the rich man's table, the dogs would come and lick his open sores. Finally, the poor man died and was carried by the angels to be with Abraham. The rich man also died and was buried, and his soul went to the place of the dead.'"

In the original Greek of Luke's Gospel, the place of the dead was called *hades*. This passage offers important insights into what happens to us when we die. Lazarus was moved out of his broken down, dilapidated house of a body by a crew of angels. They brought him to a place where the Jewish patriarch Abraham (esteemed in the Old Testament as "the friend of God") had found a home after leaving this world. To say that Lazarus was with Abraham was the same as saying that Lazarus was with God. The audience who first listened to Jesus tell this story would have clearly understood that wherever Abraham was, there God was as well.

The story continues:

Luke 16:23b
"There, in torment, he [the rich man] saw Abraham in the far distance with Lazarus at his side."

The rich man could see across the chasm; he could see across eternity. Here again, the Bible indicates that when our spirits leave our bodies they land in a specific conscious place. Lazarus landed in a place of joy, life and peace. The rich man, conversely, found himself in a place of desperate torment, and worse; it was a place from which can be seen the wonder of Heaven without any hope of moving there.

This text tells us, once more, that when we die in Christ, we move immediately to paradise.

But what about the spiritual bodies that Paul talks about?

1 Corinthians 15:42-44
"It is the same way with the resurrection of the dead. Our earthly bodies are planted in the ground when we die, but they will be raised to live forever. Our bodies are buried in brokenness, but they will be raised in glory. They are buried in weakness, but they will be raised in strength. They are buried as natural human bodies, but they will be raised as spiritual bodies. For just as there are natural bodies, there are also spiritual bodies."

Our spirit is removed in a conscious, wonderful experience with Jesus at the moment of our passing. The fact that this is true does not in any way diminish the companion truth that our spiritual body will be rehoused in a new resurrection body. The resurrection is as certain a truth as any other proclaimed in Scripture.

If the Bible is the inspired Word of God, if the Resurrection of Jesus is literally true, then it must also be the case that the followers of Christ will also receive new resurrection bodies, just as He has.

The resurrected Jesus is the "first fruit" in God's plan of redemption and restoration. "The Word become flesh," He was born to a woman in Bethlehem. The body into which His eternal *persona* was poured in that extraordinary process was as vulnerable as ours; His body would be nailed to the Cross, and eventually, He died.

On the third day following His death, Jesus reappeared in a new, resurrection body. It was similar to the original, but also significantly different. Mysteriously, the resurrected body of Jesus could defy the known material laws of the created order (appearing and disappearing seemingly supernaturally) and yet live within them (for instance, eating a meal with His disciples). His resurrection body could be felt and touched—and bore the scars of the original physical body (as Thomas would discover)—and still it seemed to walk through walls. It is a body we cannot fully understand or comprehend; but a body like it is promised to us as well.

When I die in Christ, will I fall asleep in the ground until I am given this new resurrection body, or will I immediately be translated into a new, wonderful, fully conscious reality? The answer? You will be translated into a new, wonderful, fully conscious reality with Jesus.

We need to remember that God exists outside of time, while we are presently confined to a time continuum. We live on a kind of timeline—a chronology with a beginning and an end. God has no beginning and no end; He has no past or future; He is always in the present tense. We have a past, we have a future and we pass through the present.

Imagine the timeline of history like a straight line.

If this line can represent all of time—all of history—place the beginning of history on the left end. "In the beginning, God created. . . ." Somewhere near that left end of the beginning, we can place Eden, Adam and Eve, and the rest of the early narratives in Genesis. At the other end—the end of time—on the right side—we can imagine the return of Christ, the Second Coming (as we have dubbed His return, differentiating it from His first coming in Bethlehem's manger), "the end of the age" and all that His return entails.

We exist, then, somewhere in between on that line. Perhaps, we are closer to the right end of the line than the left; perhaps, we are near the middle. No one but the Father in Heaven can know; He alone knows the calendar of the end.

Our perspectives are, naturally, bound by our sense of time. It is hard for us to step outside of time and grasp eternity. I know I had a chocolate chip cookie for breakfast this morning (yes, for breakfast—some have donuts, I had a cookie—oh yes, and some yogurt, too); that moment of abandon is somewhere to the left of where I sit now on the timeline. If I have another cookie tonight, that will be to the right of where I sit now.

How does God see my progression along the line? He is not on the line; He can see it all at once. I can see only where I have been and where I am in the minute.

We're preoccupied with where we are on the timeline. We want to know, what if I die part of the way through the timeline? What happens between the time that I die and the end of the age when Jesus returns, creates a new perfect order and destroys all the brokenness of this world? What happens to me if I die long before that Second Coming? We can only imagine the sequence, the linear order of events from our perspective on the line.

God and the eternity to which He calls us are not similarly bound, though. From Heaven's perch, the whole line can be seen at once. He sees all of history as we see the line on the page—or all four edges of the book you now hold in your hand. He understands the sequential order of our continuum and relates to us in this life through that lens; but, when we reach eternity, we will see (and somehow experience) a world without time. There is no clock ticking in Heaven. It is a place where, as the old hymn says, "time shall be no more."

I realize this can be an obtuse concept, but the original question before us presumes a linear progression. From our vantage point, it would seem that when we die we go immediately to be with the Lord, but also that we must wait to receive our resurrection bodies until the timeline plays out and Jesus returns. But is it possible that when we die, we fall out of time and become part of another order of present tense, in which our material concepts of before and after evaporate?

In Exodus 3:13-14, when Moses asks God to declare Who He is—"Whom shall I say is sending me?" to confront Pharaoh—God says He is "I Am Who I Am" I Am: the present tense, the state of being, the simultaneous, continuous, without past or future, the Eternal One not bound by time. When we die, we go to be with Him. The timeline may then be irrelevant to us; its relevance is limited only to those still on the line.

Those who are still living and remain at the Second Coming—those still living in time—will see Jesus return and the see resurrection unfold before their eyes. Whether we get our new bodies here or off the timeline is not exactly clear. We can only wonder.

What is clear is that you will get a new body, and it will be perfect.

I believe we will receive a body like the bodies in which Adam and Eve lived before sin corrupted creation and introduced death in the first place. I think, also, they will be bodies crafted by God to maximize our experience of eternity.

In the Seattle church I called home for all of my life before moving to Indiana, it was the custom to honor great souls who had gone on to glory before us with portraits, placed throughout the building, together with plaques of testimony. Consequently, when you walk into the front foyer of the Fairview Church, you will find two large paintings staring down from the wall, one on either side. To your left: Lawrence Tiffany Flynt—a towering figure and pastor in the congregation's history, a great and good man. To your right: John E. Worthen, Sr.—another man of God, a layman who poured His life into the church's ministry as well. And, oh yes, he is my grandfather, too. On other walls you'll find the likenesses of Ed Deringer, Wilbur Skaggs and so on, each with a story to tell of the Lord's faithfulness.

In the years I served as pastor of that local church (in which I was also privileged to have been raised), a small controversy developed following the passing of Iva Devine. Iva was a stalwart in the church's history, loved deeply and respected greatly. Iva was old enough to be my mother; she had a daughter the same age as I, with whom I spent many years in Sunday school. In Iva's later years, she courageously battled cancer, inspiring all who knew her. She died in her 70s.

Iva had moved to Seattle from Washington's Yakima Valley decades before. She was a young woman when she arrived in the big city, years before I was born. Upon her death, the church elected to place a portrait of Iva in the church library, bearing witness to her journey with Christ and preserving her testimony for future generations to consider. Her family was invited to submit a photograph from which an oil painting might be created.

I remember well the day the photograph of Iva Devine arrived on my desk for the portrait. It was a photograph taken when she was in her 20s, stunningly beautiful, striking really. I stared at the picture, studying it carefully. Yes, I could see it was Iva, but it was not the Iva that I knew—or that any of us knew. We knew her as a distinguished, older woman, not the demure, film-star quality image captured in this frame.

Which Iva would we memorialize? Which image would tell her story? Would we opt for the Iva of her later years or the Iva of her youth? The dialog raged for a few days; in the end, young Iva prevailed. The portrait perfectly replicated the family photo.[2]

The whole episode made me wonder, though. At what age will I be represented in my resurrection body? I'm in my 50s now. If I die today, will I be outfitted with a 50-something resurrection body? Is that my eternity? Living in my 50s isn't so bad, but honestly, given the choice, I'm voting for Jim Lyon at 27; that was a very good year.

Of course, my concerns are absurd. My resurrection body will be exactly what it needs to be, mysteriously bearing resemblance to my original body and, at the same time, like the Lord's resurrection body, perfectly formed and better. Perhaps I will see myself someday in a body that is what might have been if Eden had not been lost.

If you die in Christ, you will immediately be in the presence of Jesus, surrounded by people you once knew in this life and meeting people you have only heard about.

"Today you will be with me in paradise."

And, somehow, in some way, you will also receive a new body, perfect and without flaw.

Job knew that he, too, would live again.

> **Job 19:25-27**
> *"But as for me, I know that my Redeemer lives, and He will stand upon the earth at last. And after my body has decayed, yet in my body I will see God! I will see Him for myself. Yes, I will see Him with my own eyes. I am overwhelmed at the thought!"*

And so is the promise for all who have died in Christ. These truths do not work for those who are outside of Christ. Today, before you turn the page, you can take a moment to ask God to make things right.

Confess your sin, choose to turn away from that which you know is wrong (repent), and ask God to forgive you, giving you a new start (to be born again), understanding that God's favor is available to you because of what Jesus has done on the Cross. It's that simple to find peace with God—and the promise of life everlasting.

With that promise in hand, you will be free to explore and embrace life here and now, knowing that when you die in Christ, an even better chapter will unfold.

Question 6

Choice and Destiny: Free Will and Predestination

"If God knows what I am going to do before I do it, how can I have free will? Isn't my life pre-ordained?"

My mom and I are very close. Her name is Mildred Lyon.[1] She has spent a lifetime investing in me, and I thank God for her (and my dad, too) every night before I sleep.

My mother knows me well and, like most moms, seems to have always had an uncanny sense of what her son was going to do before he did it. For example, she knows I love chocolate, dark chocolate especially. Perhaps, the word love is not properly used in this case; obsession might be closer to the mark. As a child, my mother knew intuitively that I could not resist an open bag of Nestlé's Semi-sweet dark chocolate morsels. Actually, the bag did not have to even be open. If I knew there was a bag of the chocolate chips stored somewhere in the house, I'd find it—and eat it, too. I mean I would eat the whole bag. And yes, I went through an adolescent weight-problem phase.

My mother understood that if she wanted to bake chocolate chip cookies, she would be wise to hide the chocolate chip bags until she was ready to bake with them. By the time I was aged 13, she was stowing bags of Nestles in the strangest places: in the linen closet off the main hallway bath, in the guest bedroom dresser drawer, behind cans of Brussels sprouts and other nobody-wants-to-eat-them vegetables in the pantry. But alas, my antennae were finely tuned, and no chocolate chip escaped my notice. Sherlock Holmes had nothing on me when it came to sniffing out the trail. If my mom wasn't home, I'd break open the bag and eat my way through an episode of that creepy soap opera, *Dark Shadows*, after school. Not much healthy about either pursuit.

Mildred Lyon knew I was drawn to the chocolate; she knew chocolate could not be left out in the open at home. She knew that I struggled to resist, and she could predict my weakness. Did her knowledge of my vice make her culpable? Did she compel me to eat the Nestles? Did she "fore-ordain" that I should be weak-kneed in the face of the temptation, collapsing into the siren arms of the crinkly yellow bag with red letters? Did her all-too-accurate assessment of my predictable choices rob me of my free will, or did it just prove she was my mom?

Is *knowing* equivalent to *causing*?

My mother wrestles with some of her own demons, too. She has a fondness for See's Candy. On Mother's Day, for instance, I have often ordered her a one-pound box of See's Chocolate. She feigns surprise, but she is not. She knows me too well. And I know her, too. She thinks I don't know that the box of See's will be positioned next to her chair (not my dad's) in their family room, where she can discreetly pluck out her favorites. But I know.

And, because I know she will devour the whole box (no, she has never had a weight problem), does that mean I have predestined her to do so?

Americans spend huge sums to honor their mothers on Mother's Day. I annually invest in a box of See's; you probably have a Mother's Day routine, too. As a culture, we will try and prove our love for mom in several ways; here's a précis of the data:

- $1.9 billion. That's how much Americans spend each year buying flowers for mom on Mother's Day. That's a lot of roses, carnations, hyacinths and hydrangeas. Your mother knew you would do it. Did she make you buy those flowers, or did you choose to buy them?
- $2.9 billion. That's the amount of money we spend taking mom out to eat on Mother's Day. Is your mother making you take her to Olive Garden because she knows that's what you will do?

- $7.1 billion. This is the amount Americans will spend buying luxury gifts for their moms on Mother's Day. A day spa. Some perfume. Jewelry. The kinds of things she will not buy for herself. You might surprise her with something in this category, but she knows you're going to get her something. Are you purchasing a gift because of your own free will or because she knows you will?[2]

Billions of dollars invested in Mother's Day, this year and every year. It's all predictable, in a way. Predestined? Or by choice?

And this is the calculus we must also use to answer this question: Because God knows everything, does that mean He causes everything? Because He knows us so well, does that mean He has predetermined our choices? Does His prophetic knowledge necessarily preempt our free will?

Looking at Scripture, we must first establish the fact that God knows the future. The questions assume God already knows what is going to happen.

We believe in a God of three *omni's*. *Omni* is an original root in English meaning "all." We believe in an *omni*potent God: all powerful. We believe in an *omni*present God: always and everywhere present. And we believe in an *omni*scient God: all-knowing.

But is He really omniscient? Is He really all knowing?

Genesis 1:1
"In the beginning God created the heavens and the earth."

One of the most famous lines in all of literature, this is the beginning of God's revelation to man on the printed page. At the very get-go, God created everything. This encompasses the whole of the material order. Time began. Life began. The material order of the universe was set in motion. He made everything—the Heavens above, the earth below—all of it. It is a comprehensive summary: God is the Creator, the Author, the Source of all. It is very appropriate, very logical, very sensible to draw from this passage the conclusion that the Maker of everything understands everything.

If you make something, you understand it better than anyone else who subsequently uses it or experiences it. You know its inner workings. You know its components or ingredients. You know its properties. You know the way its constituent parts relate, one to another. The maker is the one who has superior knowledge, complete knowledge, of that which is made. Here we have the story of the beginning of everything, disclosed in the revelation of God, and in this story we have a truth: God knows everything because He made everything.

> **Matthew 10:29**
> *"What is the price of two sparrows—one copper coin? But not a single sparrow can fall to the ground without your Father knowing it. And the very hairs on your head are numbered."*

In this vast creation of God, about which He knows everything, He has both a macro and a micro grasp of what has been, what is and what will be. He possesses both a global, big-picture view, and a precise, detailed up-close-and-personal view, as well. He is conscious of the machinery of the universe even as He is conscious of a sparrow and the hairs on our heads.

If the word of Jesus can be trusted, then right now, every bird in space and time, between where I sit in Indiana and where you sit reading this book, is known and watched individually by God. He knows which birds are in the air, which are in the bush and which are being stalked by your neighbor's cat. He knows which has fallen to the ground. He knows all the details. Jesus even goes on in the passage to say that God even knows the number of hairs on our heads (a more complex census for some of us than others).

This dimension of knowledge is not static; it is a constantly changing variable. If you're like me, the number of hairs on your head is different today than it was yesterday or will likely be tomorrow.

God knows everything. He made everything. He has complete knowledge of even the tiniest details within His creation.

> **Psalm 33:13-15**
> *"The LORD looks down from heaven*
> *and sees the whole human race.*
> *From his throne he observes*
> *all who live on the earth.*
> *He made their hearts,*
> *so he understands everything they do."*

He not only knows about the birds, He knows about us. We may be able to see only the circles of life and relationships close to us. We may have knowledge of events and opportunities and disappointments within our circle of friends and family. Headlines may introduce us to the knowledge of some beyond our immediate circle. And, while I can describe what my wife wore to work today or how my granddaughter's two-year-old vocabulary is expanding, I could not presume to know about you and your world. I'm certain I do not know even all that concerns the worlds of my own four sons. None of us can come close to the knowledge of humanity everywhere on the planet that the Psalmist here claims for God. None of us can know what troubles, what motivates, or what thrills each human heart.

But God can. He has a vantage point that is unlike any other, peering from the edge of Heaven. God is in a position where He can, without the turning of His head, see the whole human race. In one glance, in one snapshot, He sees us all. Not only does He see us, He understands us. Our Maker did not just design our lungs, our brains and our hearts; He imagined and breathed into being our spirits, our souls. He made us; He knows us. Intimately. Completely.

> **Hebrews 4:13**
> *"Nothing in all creation is hidden from God. Everything is naked and exposed before his eyes, and he is the one to whom we are accountable."*

Everything is naked before His eyes. The Bible here speaks of a kind of vulnerability, doesn't it? Everything is exposed. There is no shadow, there is no curtained corner beyond His view—everything is seen. Intellectually, we understand that God always sees us, but practically we do not always conduct ourselves as if we believe it. We imagine that if we do not look at Him, He will not look at us.

Have you ever gone to the mall to shop in a hurry? Running late, you run to your car, jump in, and drive off, hoping to pick up a Mother's Day card before the rest of your day begins. As soon as you check the rearview mirror, you know you're a mess. Your hair is chaos, your face unshaven. There's no time to deal with it, though—and besides, you are just planning to run in and then run out. As you walk through the mall, you see your reflection in the display window glass: the neglected ketchup stain on your sweatshirt now like neon, the denim jeans torn in all the wrong places—but that's the style these days, isn't it? You can't stop to think about how disheveled you actually look. You have an errand to run.

You walk directly into the card store and look at no one. Staring at the floor, you believe that if you don't look at anyone they will not look at you. If you do not make eye contact, you will be ignored. If you don't see them, you will not be seen.

It's a preposterous train of thought, of course. Haven't you ever seen somebody at the mall who didn't want to be seen, would not look at you and pretended they were invisible. The fact that you noticed proves they were not. Of course you have seen them. We're all observed.

In the same way, God sees us. You cannot hide. You are noticed. I am, too. All of us are. For Heaven's sake.

There is nothing hidden from Him. It is a truth is at once comforting and terrifying.

It's comforting because if I'm like the sparrow and fall, He sees me and may swoop down to save me. But it's terrifying because if I go places I should not go or do things I should not do, I can never escape His gaze.

That's why He has the capacity to judge us. It's why He is the One to Whom we are accountable. He sees everything. He will not have to call any witnesses to the bench on the judgment day. He is the witness. He has seen it all. Everything. Already.

> **Matthew 6:4, 18**
> *"Give your gifts in private, and your Father, who sees everything, will reward you."*
>
> *"Then no one will notice that you are fasting, except your Father, who knows what you do in private. And your Father, who sees everything, will reward you."*

Even though you attempt to act in secret—quietly, discreetly, privately—God "sees everything" You cannot hide anything from God. He sees all the good, and He sees all the bad. He will reward you based upon the deeds you have done. It's all based on His ability to know us and to know everything about us.

Psalm 139:2-4

"You know when I sit down or stand up.
You know my thoughts even when I'm far away.
You see me when I travel
and when I rest at home.
You know everything I do.
You know what I am going to say
even before I say it, LORD."

Here we have an expansion on what He knows. So far, it could be interpreted that God knows only where I am today. But here we see that God knows where I'm going to be before I arrive. He knows what I am going to say before I say it. He can understand where I'll be tomorrow, before I know where I'll be tomorrow.

This passage and others like it introduce the concept that God sees not only where we are and where we have been—He sees our future course, as well. He knows what I'm going to say at dinner tonight. I don't know what I'm going to say. He knows what I'm going to wear tomorrow. I'm not even sure where I'll be tomorrow.

Psalm 139:16

"You saw me before I was born.
Every day of my life was recorded in your book.
Every moment was laid out
before a single day had passed."

It's astonishing really, a phenomenal premise: every day of my life recorded, in advance. Of course, it's natural to come to the conclusion after reading these verses that if God already knows what's going to come to pass, then am I really free to make my own choices? Are we not, therefore, simply drones, pawns, robots? If every day is already mapped out, what choices are left for us to make?

Isaiah 49:1

"Listen to me, all you distant lands!
Pay attention, you who are far away!
The LORD called me before my birth;
from within my womb He called me by name."

Here is my paraphrase of that passage: God knew my name even before I was delivered into my mother's arms. When I was still a fetus curled up in my mother's womb, He was whispering to me. He was calling me, by name, "Isaiah. Isaiah."

God created the world and understands how it functions. He knows everything about the present—the birds in the air and the hairs on our heads. He knows everything about the future—what we're going to say before we say it. And God knows our past—He knew us before we were formed in the womb.

If He knows all that already, is there really room to maneuver? Do we really have any options?

The clue that informs our answer is this: Isaiah was called. It's the call of God, the invitation of God. It's a choice, an invitation to which we choose to respond. From the beginning, He has whispered into our hearts, even when we were not able to understand very well, even when we could not hear very well. He has marked us and called to us. He has invited us to make a choice.

> **Deuteronomy 30:19-20**
> *"Today I have given you the choice between life and death, between blessings and curses. Now I call on heaven and earth to witness the choice you make. Oh, that you would choose life, so that you and your descendants might live! You can make this choice by loving the Lord your God, obeying him, and committing yourself firmly to him. This is the key to your life. And if you love and obey the Lord, you will live long in the land the Lord swore to give your ancestors Abraham, Isaac, and Jacob."*

Moses, near the end of his days, is speaking to his people. He's freed them from slavery in Egypt, parted the Red Sea, and led them on a journey through a desert wilderness for 40 years. He's preparing them for a new future in the Promised Land, and what does he say to them?

You have a choice. As Moses speaks, God already knows how the people will choose. Does that mean that He made their choices? Does the knowledge of something predetermine a certain outcome? Because I know something about you, does that mean I caused you to be how you are? Chocolate chips, anyone?

If you take these texts together with the rest of Scripture, there are some truths you can uncover.

First, God does know everything. He is completely omniscient. He knows the before, the present, and the after. God is not still learning things. He is not still discovering new things. He is not discovering who you are as your life unfolds and you make choices. He is not waiting for you to decide what you are going to do tonight before you go home from work, or what you're going to eat for dinner in order to find out what will happen next. He already knows. If this were not true, He would be greatly diminished. If He does not already know, He is on our plane, learning as He goes, just like we are.

God is not like us in this. He has complete knowledge all at once. God's knowledge is not dependent on His creation. We are not in a position to disclose anything to Him. God's knowledge is not based on what we do. He is ahead of us.

The knowledge of God is based not only on how things are and will be but also on what would be and could be. He knows not only how things are, but how things could be if we chose differently. He knows it all, and He knows it all at a glance.

God knows about everything in the world. He knows the whole course of history and where the next cyclone will be. He knows where the next triumph and the next tragedy will take place. He is two steps ahead. His knowledge encompasses the whole world and your journey specifically.

And, as we saw in the last chapter, God knows all of this because He exists outside of time.

Once more, imagine this line as the unfolding experience of the material order. At the far left is the very beginning of creation and the far right is the end of the age, when all things will be made new. We are presently somewhere on this line, between the beginning and the end.

We are finite. We can only keep track of two parts of the timeline: the present circumstances of our social circle of friends and some world political leaders through the news, and an informed understanding of the world's history. We are capable of knowing what is to the left of us. The space to the right of us on the line is impossible to predict with certainty.

God, however, is not bound by the timeline. He is the creator. He made the line and the paper and the ink and exists not on the page but off the page. His relationship to the line is much like your relationship to it as a reader of this book. He exists outside of time. He sits back and, just as you can see the whole line at once, God can see all of time at once.

He does not exist in a linear or sequential chronology; He exists within and apart from it. From Heaven's point of view, the expanse of history is, in a way, simultaneous, seen all at once.

Does that mean He causes the events that fall into place on the line to happen? Because He can see the line, all at once, has He preempted our ability to choose? Is free will—the unique gift of God to the zenith of His creation, humankind—trumped by His omniscient knowledge?

Let's change the illustration a little bit. Instead of saying that the line represents all of time, let's say that it represents just your life. Or, instead, let's say it represents my life.

My life begins on the left, it will end on the right. It is my conviction that human life begins at conception, when a woman's egg is fertilized by a man's sperm. In this transaction, the complete DNA mapping of life is present, from cell one, which quickly subdivides into two and so on. God breathed life into the womb; in time, I was born. My line, then, in my view, begins with conception at the far left end.

I was conceived out of wedlock. My parents-by-blood were both Irish nationals; I am an Irishman by birth. My birthfather, imprisoned by the British because of his involvement with the Irish Republican Army and my birthmother, born and raised in the Gaeltacht (that far part of western Ireland where the Irish language has always been spoken first; where Gaelic, not English, is the norm) found themselves in circumstances in which it was not possible to care for me. I was relinquished for adoption while still an infant.

Ultimately, I was adopted by Don and Mildred Lyon. Seattle became my home. I attended Webster Elementary, just blocks away from the dramatic cliffs of Sunset Hill, overlooking Shilshole Bay. I graduated from Ingraham High School and went on to earn a bachelor's degree from Seattle Pacific University. Next, I entered the University of Washington Law School.

After leaving law school, I landed a job with Northwest Airlines. Along the way, I ran for public office and, for a brief term, represented 74,000 people in northwest Seattle in the Washington State Legislature. As legislative district boundaries were redrawn, I left the House and eventually became a pastor. I married. I became the father of four sons.

I moved to Indiana. I started speaking on the radio. Now I'm writing a book. All of these events can be placed somewhere on my timeline, moving from left to right. I cannot know what will happen next.

As I look at my timeline, I know God has seen it all from before the beginning. Before the foundation of the world, Ephesians 1 tells me that God knew me and predestined me to be adopted into His family. He can see the rest of my timeline, which I cannot now see. But does that mean that God has been the cause, the author of each of the events named above?

Let's go back to my beginning. I was conceived out of wedlock. Two persons, not married, brought me to life. I have subsequently met them; they are good people, who found themselves in a very complicated world. Some choices were made.

Did God know that would happen?

Yes.

Did God cause that to happen?

No. The relationship necessary to conceive me was outside of God's design for human sexuality; sexual relationships are, by God's design, reserved for marriage. Sexual relationships outside of a marriage union are forbidden. The Scripture tells us that God never tempts us to sin. My birthparents made their own choices.

Did He know that I would be relinquished?

Yes.

Did He force my biological mother to put me up for adoption?

No. She chose to do so.

The fact that I know the sun will rise tomorrow does not mean I will cause the sun to rise. The fact that my mother knows I'll eat every bag of chocolate chips I can find does not mean she has caused me to do so. That fact that God can see down the road past where we are does not mean He has robbed us of the right to choose. Knowledge is not a synonym for cause.

We have free will within the context of God's knowledge.

Did God know me from before the foundation of the world?

Yes.

Did He compel my birthparents to become sexually active outside of marriage so that I might be born?

No.

God's knowledge allows Him to supernaturally pick up the pieces of even our failures. Knowing our stumbles, He is ahead of us and able to help sort things out for the good—if we surrender our folly to Him. Even at this stage, the choice is still ours.

Did God prepare a loving family to adopt me?

Yes.

Were they compelled to do so?

No.

Did my birthmother surrender my life into God's hands?

Yes.

Was it her choice to do so?

Yes.

Did God call me to the Christian ministry?

Yes.

Was I compelled to accept the call?

No.

And so on, throughout my modest biography. God knows. God allows us to choose. We make choices. We make mistakes. He walks ahead and turns the bad for the good, when we choose to allow Him to be sovereign in our lives.

Did God know that Jesus would be betrayed by Judas?

Yes.

Did God cause Judas to betray Jesus?

No.

Can God take even the most hopeless circumstances, consequent to our own poor choices, and turn them for the good?

Yes.

Must we choose to allow Him to do so in our lives?

Yes.

Does He already know if we will cooperate with His will?

Yes.

Does He love us anyway, knowing everything there is to know about us?

Yes.

This is the miracle of amazing grace.

Romans 8:28

"And we know that God causes everything to work together for the good of those who love God and are called according to his purpose for them."

What the devil means for harm, God turns for the good. He doesn't make you choose, but if you choose to surrender to Him, He will bring your choices in congruence with His will.

I believe that God knew I was to be the pastor of the Madison Park Church in Indiana before I was conceived. I believe that God knew that I would be called to preach the Gospel before I was born. Still, I have had to make choices along the way. I was not compelled by God to make those choices; I made them myself, though He saw them before I chose.

Our redemption is fully the consequence of our choice. We choose whether or not we will be redeemed. God will not compel you to choose the right.

Woodrow Wilson once observed that it is providentially "the privilege of men everywhere to choose their own way of life and of obedience."[3] We each make the decision for ourselves, who we will become, whom we will serve, what we will do.

Where are you in your timeline? Imagine Heaven's gate. Imagine that you are now standing before the gate, and, as you do, you see this inscription from Revelation: "Whosoever will, come."

It is an invitation for anyone who chooses. Come. Enter. Welcome. It is the invitation of the New Testament. It is the Bible's close. And, as you make the decision to walk forward through the gate, you choose to be redeemed. As you look backward and see the gate behind you, you may be surprised to find that on the other side of Heaven's gate, there's another inscription that reads, "Chosen from before the foundation of the world." Both are true. And as you walk into the world as one of the chosen redeemed, know that God chose you and knows you. But only because He could see you choose too.

What will you choose? You decide.

Question 5

The Voice of God

"Some people say they are able to hear —or sense—God actually speaking to them. Is this possible? If you are asking God to speak, how can you know if God is actually speaking in reply or, alternatively, your imagination isn't just working overtime? And, can Satan get in the mix and give you the wrong answer?"

1 Samuel 3:1-10

"Meanwhile, the boy Samuel served the Lord by assisting Eli. Now in those days messages from the Lord were very rare, and visions were quite uncommon. One night Eli, who was almost blind by now, had gone to bed. The lamp of God had not yet gone out, and Samuel was sleeping in the Tabernacle near the Ark of God. Suddenly the Lord called out, 'Samuel!'

"'Yes?' Samuel replied. 'What is it?' He got up and ran to Eli. 'Here I am. Did you call me?'

"'I didn't call you,' Eli replied. 'Go back to bed.' So he did.

Then the Lord called out again, 'Samuel!'

Again Samuel got up and went to Eli. 'Here I am. Did you call me?'

"'I didn't call you, my son,' Eli said. 'Go back to bed.'

> *Samuel did not yet know the* LORD *because he had never had a message from the* LORD *before. So the* LORD *called a third time, and once more Samuel got up and went to Eli. 'Here I am. Did you call me?'*
>
> *Then Eli realized it was the* LORD *who was calling the boy. So he said to Samuel, 'Go and lie down again, and if someone calls again, say, "Speak,* LORD *, your servant is listening."' So Samuel went back to bed.*
>
> *And the Lord came and called as before, 'Samuel! Samuel!'*
>
> *And Samuel replied, 'Speak, your servant is listening.'"*

This text substantiates, as do others, the claim that, yes indeed, God can speak to us in a voice that can be heard. Yes, God does speak. Yes, God speaks in a way He can be understood.

When you approach Scripture, it's important to make a decision about how you believe it most authentically can influence your life. One approach recognizes the Bible as simply a record of ancient events (or even an anthology of fable-like lessons grounded in truth) that is not (or cannot be) replicated in the here and now. The biblical narrative, then, represents chapters and dispensations closed in history. Because we now have the written record of those events, we are no longer privy to, we should no longer expect, and we can no longer access the kind of supernatural phenomena described. Those phenomena are closed to us now. There are truths to be grasped by this analysis, to be sure, but it assumes that the intervening supernatural will not be experienced by us here and now.

Another approach suggests that the Bible is more than history (although grounded in history) and that it is a living Word defining God's activity then and now. You can choose to believe that the Scriptures expose a dynamic of relationship between the Creator and His creation that is both a reflection of and a template for all ages. With this in mind, Bible stories are testimonies that suggest replication in our present day. Under this rubric, the Bible presents a God who does not change and whose relational matrix with humanity, the zenith of His creation, does not change either—what people experienced with God in the past tense can be experienced by us in the present tense.

Choosing either of these approaches to the Bible-as-a-guide is necessarily an exercise in faith. I have landed in the latter category, not the former.

If I own the premise that God's love, care, justice, power-for-the-good, and goodwill are fixed and unchanging, that these characteristics are proved true in the experience of humanity recorded long ago in the Bible, then it is sensible to also own the premise that He will express these dimensions of His persona today as He did yesterday. It is logical to expect that God will interface with us now as He did with men and women way back then.

Consequently, I approach the Bible as a document that discloses to me a pattern and methodology to embrace in my present day experience. I do not imagine that I will experience all of the things experienced by great men and women of Scripture; not everyone who lived in the age of Moses, for instance, heard the voice of God in a burning bush that was not consumed. But I do imagine that it's possible, at some important moments, for me to experience some of them; even as the Apostle Paul understood God's calling to Europe in a dream (see Acts 16), so might I. And, out of all the supernatural experiences recorded in Scripture, none is more common than God speaking into the human heart.

> **Matthew 7:7-8**
> *"Keep on asking, and you will receive what you ask for. Keep on seeking, and you will find. Keep on knocking, and the door will be opened to you. For everyone who asks, receives. Everyone who seeks, finds. And to everyone who knocks, the door will be opened."*

This is an invitation, clear and concise, powerfully stated and restated in the same passage, for us to speak to God. It's Jesus speaking, inviting us to seek a reply, an answer, an intervention from God. If we seek, we will find. The speaking of God into our unique circumstances and into our individual lives is at the core of Jesus' famous call to search and pursue.

> **James 1:5-8**
> *"If you need wisdom, ask our generous God, and he will give it to you. He will not rebuke you for asking. But when you ask Him, be sure that your faith is in God alone. Do not waiver, for a person with divided loyalty is as unsettled as a wave of the sea that is blown and tossed by the wind. Such people should not expect to receive anything from the Lord. Their loyalty is divided between God and the world, and they are unstable in everything they do."*

Here is another invitation from God to seek, in this case, His wisdom. It is also a promise: Ask God and He will reply. If we dabble with God, seeking Heaven's answer with uncertainty, doubt, and mixed allegiances, then we will be frustrated and even more uncertain in the end. We will have difficulty discerning His answer because of our own vacillation—up and down, all over the map, afraid to trust completely. But, if we are determined to find God's wisdom, approaching Him with sure-footed certainty that He will not be deaf to our plea, then He will speak in reply, somehow, someway.

In each of these New Testament passages there is a uniform voice, a pattern and a promise. God is in the business of communicating.

At the beginning of this chapter, I cited the Old Testament story of the boy Samuel, an episode that predates the coming of Christ into the world. Samuel's call came centuries before Jesus or James could be heard in the first century of the Christian era. No one knows exactly when Samuel was born, but he probably lived in the late 12th century or early 11th century (before Christ). In those centuries before "the Word became flesh and dwelt among us," this same God was interacting—communicating—with His people. In this page from history, God spoke to Samuel. It would not be the last time He did so.

God spoke to Samuel so powerfully, with such vividness, that Samuel was awakened from sleep. No one else hears the voice, but Samuel does. He hears from His Maker. He does not know to whom he is listening, and he mistakes the call for that of his caretaker and guardian, Eli. But it is, unmistakably in the end, the voice of God.

All of us would do well to acknowledge we have a thirst to hear from God. The reason this question is even posed is that we each have an innate, native hunger for communion with—communication with—God. We need to hear from Him because we long to be recognized by Him, to be noticed, to be understood, to be protected.

We long to be recognized in general. If we walk into a room and are ignored, admit it or not, we feel diminished. When visiting a church building or a coffee shop or a retail store, we hope to be acknowledged in some way. If we feel invisible, we are unlikely to return. If no one speaks to us, nods to us, even looks at us, then we wonder, "What's wrong with me?" or "What's wrong with them?" We all are wired for relationship, and we emotionally and intellectually wither if isolated and alone.

A woman in the local church where I serve as pastor once called me, perturbed and with an edge in her voice. She was disturbed by the way she was greeted on a Sunday morning—too many people were greeting her. She was greeted in the parking lot, she was greeted at the front door, she was greeted in the foyer and as she entered the auditorium. The last straw seemed to be that, after finally finding her seat inside, someone seated near her greeted her, too. She complained, "Can't I just come and worship God without being greeted?!" She apparently wanted to worship God alone and be left alone. Wrong church.

There are times when I want to be alone with God, too. And, at the end of each of our Sunday services, we invite people to step to the front and kneel before God in prayer. We designate one half of the kneeling benches that arc across the front of our auditorium at the foot of the platform for "private and personal prayer only; no one will bother you, just you and the Lord, alone." The other half of the kneeling benches are reserved for those who would like to pray with someone; persons kneeling there will be met by a prayer partner, prepared to share and lift their requests to Heaven with them.

Hearing this woman's frustration, it occurred to me that we should also set aside a section of seats in the auditorium for loners, posted, perhaps, with a sign at the end of each row: "Leave me alone!" Welcome: just sit over here, and you'll be ignored.

In the end, of course, we have not designated seating in this way, because most of us want to hear from someone else, to know we've been noticed. Nothing satisfies our need for acknowledgment more directly, more completely than the sense that someone has spoken to us. All of us have the need to be noticed by God.

Fundamentally, we want to be reassured that God is there, that He is, that He cares and is willing to do something about it. In a complex and often troublesome world, we want God to give us direction so that we will know what to do. We need to be comforted with a soothing word every now and then—a healing balm from the Lord. We long for an encouraging word, as from a parent, affirming our worth and value.

We thirst for these things. Admit this to yourself. It's a step toward hearing.

Yesterday I went and bought a few impatiens. I like impatiens, flowers that flourish in the humid, subtropical summers of Indiana. After you plant them, all you have to do is water them and they grow. You don't have to deadhead them, pinching withered blooms, separate them as they spread, fuss over them in any way. They just keep blooming and blooming as long as you water them and the sun shines. I like pink and white impatiens best, but I was a little late in the season this year and red was all that was left at my local nursery. I picked up a flat of weary red impatiens for my backyard. It was a hot day and they hadn't been watered on the nursery shelf for some time. Without water, impatiens can quickly become a shriveling, limp, shadow-of-its-better-self, a pitiful spectre near death. Moist tubular plants, impatiens thirst like no others.

I planted those red, near-death, pathetic plants in my yard and watered them after dark. In the morning: Voila! The red impatiens stood proudly, reborn, as if never thirsty before. An astonishing recovery, really, sudden and dramatic. Beautiful.

This is an exact representation of who we are and how we can live. If we do not hear from God, if we are not watered by His voice for a season, we become thirsty, spiritually limp. We feel detached, confused, discouraged. But just a word from the Lord, just a moment in which you realize that He knows who you are and where you are, and life springs back; we begin to stand tall and bloom once more. Even if our circumstances remain unchanged, even if we still have tall mountains to climb, hearing God speak empowers and invigorates us, like a tall glass of water for a thirsty soul.

Admit your thirst. Own it.

If I am honest and admit I am desperate for the voice of God in my life, will He speak? Does He speak to people like me?

Yes. He spoke to Samuel. He called Samuel by name. God has the capacity to speak. From a biblical perspective, there's no doubt about that. Still, there are seasons when God is quiet. There are seasons when we do not hear from Him or find it difficult to identify His voice in the din all around us.

I don't know why He might choose to be silent at times. I believe He always has my well-being at heart. He may know that if He speaks now, I won't listen later. Maybe He knows I'm too busy and, if He spoke, I would not take the time to digest what He has to say. Maybe He knows I'm not ready to hear what He has to say, because my heart is, in some way, unwilling to accept any word that challenges its predetermined options or conclusions. Or perhaps there are circumstances that must yet come into play, and until they do, He cannot disclose, knowing that His word would bring only more confusion until more pieces of the puzzle are on the table for us to see. There are all kinds of reasons God, caring for us, might choose to be silent for a time.

He knows so much more than I know. He has so much more understanding of my world than I have . . . and of my heart, too. Because of that, I have to accept that there may be seasons, there may be moments, there may be long lapses of time during which He does not speak because He knows best.

So it was in the days of Samuel, it seems, when messages from God were few and far between. But even in those moments, I would suggest that there is a presence of God that can be known even when His voice cannot be heard. It's that almost inarticulate sense that God is with me. I can be calm when I have no right to be calm. I can be steady when everything in my life gives me reasonable excuse to be unsteady. There is just a sense of His Presence, even if there is not a word. Be still and know.

If I do ask God for something, if I do speak to Him or He does speak back to me, how do I know that I'm really hearing from Him?

This is one of the trickiest questions in all of human experience. We all have active imaginations. Have you ever had a conversation with someone in your mind? Have you ever had a conversation with someone who wasn't there? Are you introverted like me? An introvert is, among other things, a person who processes things internally and not externally. In other words, I have all kinds of conversations in my head with people who aren't there. I answer questions. I offer questions. I debate, sing songs, agree, disagree, and all the rest, but all inside my head. If you were to look at me, you might think me a zombie, out of touch with the world around me, when in fact my mind is racing constantly. Introverts process internally, speaking naturally only when they have drawn a conclusion.

Conversely, an extrovert processes things externally, reaching conclusions by speaking out loud and sometimes even if alone. Introversion is not superior to or less than extroversion; both are natural and reasonable processes; we're just wired in different ways. But if you're introverted like me, it can be even more difficult to discern whether the voice in your head is actually a communication from God or a manifestation of your capacity to fabricate a conversation to get an answer.

Sometimes I get answers from God that grieve or frighten me. I am then tempted to think, "Well it must be from God because it is not an answer I like, and I deserve to be uncomfortable, to be disciplined, to be punished" or whatever. At other times, I may believe God has given me a sweet reply, and I interpret it this way: "Well, that can't be right, that can't be what God intends because I deserve to be uncomfortable, to be disciplined, to be punished, etc." Do you catch the refrain? I deserve to be unhappy. This becomes the quirky and flawed measure of our approach to divine communication.

After admitting that you have a thirst to hear from God, the next step is to admit that God loves you. He cares for you, deeply. He wants you to be whole. He desires to adopt you into His own family. He wants to redeem you from the devil's business. His ambition is not to cause you grief or subtract from your life. That's hell's object, not Heaven's. God is interested in breathing life into you. Full and free. He wants what's best for you. He wants to call the best out of you.

Do you want to hear from God? Approach Him believing He is for you, not against you.

You need to also approach God with a clear conscience—or with the intent of clearing your conscience. If you're nurturing sin, harboring a grudge, holding on to something you know is not right or refusing to do what you already know is right, then conversation with God will be severely compromised. Clean it up. Make a decision to repent—change course—and humble yourself before the One from whom you want to hear. Tell Him: "Lord, I'm so sorry that I did what I should not have done. I'm so sorry that I refused to do what I know I should have done." Whatever it is that haunts you, lay it down before God. And know that as you do, you do so in the name of Jesus. The blood of Jesus can cover it, remove it, cleanse it.

Shame can make us deaf. Pride drowns out the voice of God. A guilty conscience can only confuse us and impair our hearing.

Here are some accurate yardsticks by which you can gauge whether you're hearing from God or from your own imagination:

First, trust the Scripture. You need to measure what you hear in your head by the printed Word of God. If you believe God is telling you to steal what is not yours to take, the Scripture will help clarify: such a voice could not be God's. He will not plant an idea in your head that contravenes His written Word. I've had married men tell me, with a straight face, that God was telling them to leave their wives and develop sexual relationships with other women because God wants them to be happy and they're not happy at home and . . . well, nonsense. Such counsel cannot come from God; the Scripture plainly forbids such conduct.

The Scripture is primary. If you want to understand God's voice, then you must be a student of the Word. Eat from it. Drink from it. Digest it. Allow it to become part of you, so that you can measure what you think and what you hear by its revealed wisdom. The Psalmist encourages us: "I have hidden your word in my heart, / that I might not sin against you" (Psalm 119:11).

Second, ask yourself if the voice you hear brings you a sense of peace. Sometimes God will speak into our lives with a very challenging word, but still, there's something about truth that ultimately brings peace. The truth always heals even when it's hard to bear. God only speaks truth. The truth may challenge us to leave our comfort zones, apologize for our errors, take a chance or move us into some danger. But if it is truly the voice of God, our quickened pulse cannot obscure "the peace that passes all understanding," the internal security of God's Presence. Is what you perceive as the voice of God bringing you calm?

Third, you can measure the voice by living in consultation with the Body of Christ, manifested in a local church. Other believers can be an objective sounding board. "This is what I think the Lord told me. How does that sound to you?" God has woven us together and can speak truth to us through community. It is not possible to discern accurately the voice of God in isolation from His family, if it is at all possible for us to interact with that family. God, in His wisdom, has called us to be brothers and sisters in a new family of His making. It is in this family of Christian relationships that He has chosen most effectively to equip us with the discerning gifts of His Holy Spirit. Never underestimate the power of the Body of Christ as a sage instrument when interpreting the different voices vying for our attention.

God spoke to Samuel, but the message he received was ultimately for Eli. This pattern is repeated throughout Scripture. Somehow, we are united and need dialog with one another to help us understand together what God is saying to us.

Can Satan get in the way and confuse us? Yes, he can.

And so, fourth: pray that God will protect you from being deceived. This is especially important when in the pursuit of some specific knowledge or direction. Pray always that the Lord will protect you from being deceived by the enemy of your soul. God will honor that promise, but you must walk forward believing that He has. That way, when you walk forward, you know that you have framed your request in this way: "Lord I'm open to whatever you have for me, but protect me from being deceived." You have to then trust that God is protecting, as you thoughtfully embrace the answer given.

When God speaks, He generally speaks to us in ways that reassure us and reveal His glory. His voice does not necessarily call us to *do* anything. Many—if not most—messages from God simply reassure us, remind us that He is working for us and so on. Sometimes His communication will carry an assignment; He may give us direction to do this or do that, to not go there or do that. Generally, however, the proof of His speaking is demonstrated over time; as we watch events unfold, His words come back to mind and He is glorified.

Learning first to listen for His voice telling us we are loved can be an important prerequisite to hearing His voice telling us what to do.

Not long ago, I went to Ukraine as radio host for the English-language program *ViewPoint* (produced by Christians Broadcasting Hope, CBH). CBH produces several different language broadcasts globally, one in Russian. The Russian CBH program has a large following in southern and eastern Ukraine. I traveled there to encourage our Russian-speaking listeners, preach in churches that were born from the broadcast in the days when Soviet atheism reigned in the area, and to produce some *ViewPoint* programs in the field, capturing the flavor of the place in a *National-Geographic*-for-Jesus kind of way. While I was there, I visited large cities and small villages—A to Z. The cities seemed to be in a recovery stage, soiled by decades of industrial development without regard for environmental impacts. The villages were a world apart, with primitive infrastructure by Western standards, almost fairy-tale like.

These little villages have a lot of charm, set in vast fields of sunflowers, canola, and the occasional forest. Dotted with Hansel-and-Gretel-like cottages, framed by bright blue shutters and geraniums in window boxes, life in the villages is, nonetheless, taxing. The farmers and their families eke out a modest living from the land, somewhere between *Little House on the Prairie* and the 20th century. Delightful and generous, the Ukrainians seemed undeterred by their hardships; they listened for God.

The aging, Soviet-era toxic industrial base of some Ukrainian cities poses different challenges for those who call them home. In the city of

Mariupol, for instance, 100,000 people are employed in various metallurgy plants producing iron. These plants spew into the sky a choking haze that can, quite literally, take your breath away. The smokestacks that pierce the horizon in every direction, along the shore of the Sea of Azoz, are without number.

As I looked across the urban landscape, obscured by airborne particulates beyond anything I could have imagined, I wondered how the hard-working and gracious Ukrainians who call the city home endure, day in and day out. My eyes burned. My throat narrowed. My lungs felt the grit.

When we left to journey on to Berlin, via Kiev, my eyes were still burning. I wear contact lenses, which magnified the irritation. On the flight from Kiev, I was forced to remove the contact from my right eye. My eyes felt like they were literally being sliced by razor blades. The pain grew. My eyes hurt open. My eyes hurt closed. They watered profusely. I could find no relief. It was the most excruciating, painful, long and drawn out plane ride of my life. The hours trapped in that plane cabin seemed like days.

Other passengers could not help but notice my weeping, running, swollen, inflamed eyes. A group of Russian tourists returning from a Black Sea resort came over to my aisle seat and tried to comfort me, thinking I was crying from some emotional trauma. My traveling friend and translator, Kelley Phillips, explained (in Russian) that he and I "had just broken up," and that's why I was weeping. Very funny. Actually, it was. I needed to smile in spite of myself.[1]

My eyes began to swell so that I wondered if I would go blind. My vision narrowed, already dim without my contacts. My entire face started to appear deformed; they called me Quasimodo. Very funny (Not really).

I didn't know what to do. I was desperate. I begged God that day. I wondered if the Ukrainians I had met ever begged God when Stalin collectivized their farms, when the Nazis invaded, when the Communists came back and ravaged the landscape "for the proletariat." I wondered if the man I had met whose whole family had been deported into the Siberian gulag, never to be seen again, when it was learned they had become Christians, ever begged God.

My struggle seemed petty in comparison, but dear-God-in-Heaven my eyes hurt so much! I asked Him what was happening? What was wrong with my eyes? What could I do? What had I done? To what had I been exposed? I need answers. Please, God. I'm trapped and in pain.

I honestly thought about hell for the first time in a new way. Hell without any prospect of relief. Suffering with no end in sight. You can endure almost anything if you know that at some point it will be over, but what if this were like hell, where you're suffering and all you can know is that it will never be over. The pain grew more intense as I tried to calculate how long I would be on the plane. At least I knew I would not be flying in this way forever. We had to land sometime. That was a help.

As the plane approached Berlin, I was reduced to despair. I had heard God speak into my life on other days. I had witnessed the astonishing intervention of God miraculously at other times. For twenty years, I had preached boldly the power of God to heal and make whole. But, in that moment—that one tortured moment—I found myself wondering if there was a God out there after all. He wasn't speaking. I could not hear.

And then God spoke to me.

This happened to me. I cannot say it will be the same for you, but it happened to me. Sometimes, God calls me by name. And, on that day, in the agony of my hapless, hopeless, despondent, devolving walk with God, I heard my name.

"Jim."

"Yes, Lord?"

"Your eyes will be fine."

"Will they, Lord? Will they be fine? Am I going to lose an eye on this trip? How will they be fine? Are you going to strike them fine? Are you going to appoint them to be fine? Take the pain away now if they're going to be fine. Please?"

"Your eyes will be fine."

That's all He gave me. I had more questions. I wanted more. But with that, the conversation ended. It was, however, enough for me to take a deep breath and just hope, believing that God was on the case.

We landed at the airport, went to the first aid station there and received some drops, and was told I needed to see an ophthalmologist right away.

"Didn't you say my eyes would be fine, Lord? I just talked to a trained medical professional who said I had to find an ophthalmologist right now. It's 9:00 P.M. in Berlin. How am I going to find an eye doctor? Still on the case, God?"

Kelley Phillips drove Quasimodo to the St. Agnes Hospital; it is not equipped to treat eye injuries. We try two other hospitals; no eye specialists on duty that night. By midnight, we had driven all over Berlin, my eyes still in severe distress, my vision fading. No hospital could be found that could provide treatment, it seemed—at least in the middle of the night. There was one hospital left: the Benjamin Franklin Hospital of Berlin. Benjamin Franklin? Berlin? I didn't have the energy to ask why the name.

In the emergency room at the Benjamin Franklin, we learned that an ophthalmologist was on call and would see me. She met me in an exam room and gave me a full eye exam. Her English was heavily accented. "Very interesting," she repeated, deadpan, without emotion, without further comment.

Through it all, I replayed the one word I had from God, clearly understood, sometimes hard to believe, but hope-giving just the same: "Your eyes are going to be fine."

Eventually, the doctor began to question me.

"Have your pupils always been different sizes?"

". . . I don't know. I don't think so."

"Have you been to an eye doctor lately?"

"Yes."

"I don't want to alarm you, but I need to have you wait here while I go in the other room because we need to discuss and decide what to do with you."

My case sounded ominous. I waited in silence for 30 minutes in the exam room, until she returned. "I need to call my superiors because I am not sure what to do with you."

Once again, I heard her say, "We don't know what to do with you."

"I've been traveling most of the day and am exhausted. Would it be safe for me to return to my hotel?"

"You need to stay here"

The refrain in my mind: "Jim, your eyes will be fine."

She left. She came back. She explained. "I have consulted with other members of our ophthalmology department. Your cornea is very inflamed and irritated. We suspect a chemical exposure as the cause. The inflammation is grotesque and obvious; it is no wonder you have been experiencing such severe pain."

She continued for a moment, but I was lost at the use of the word "grotesque." Quasimodo became my new name.

"The news is good, though." I came back around to the conversation. "It does not appear that your cornea or any other part of the eye has been permanently damaged. Your vision will return to normal within a few days.

The pupils are different sizes, we believe, because of the eye drops given at the airport. Your eyes will be fine."

She said, with a German accent, "Your eyes will be fine." God had spoken.

The doctor gave me some drops to manage the swelling and reduce the discomfort. I thanked her for her kindness and concern. We even talked briefly about God, as I acknowledged Him before her, too. I believe my visit to her office in the Benjamin Franklin Hospital of Berlin was part of a larger design in her life. God did not explain, nor could I have comprehended (nor would I have cared about what was going on in her life or why she needed to be there or why I needed to be there) the backstory, the larger story that framed the whole experience. None of that mattered to me on the plane, because my eyes hurt so desperately. God gave me what I needed to know, when I needed to know it.

Your eyes will be fine. Trust me. Relax.

The next morning I woke up and still looked like Quasimodo, but felt better. By noon, I was visibly better. By the end of the day, I was wearing contacts again. The most extraordinary dimension of the whole experience, however, was that God spoke to me. I knew He was working for my good. He noticed me. He heard me. He responded to me. The relief and empowerment of these truths overwhelmed me.

The Lord might have spoken to me otherwise. He might have said, "You're going to be blind. Look at your son (who was traveling with me) for the last time." A word from God is not always welcome news in the way that we want it to be welcome. But a word from God will give you what you need to know when you need to know it. That is enough.

Pray that He will protect you from error. Samuel did not know the Lord yet, because he had not had a message from God yet. It's curious that the knowledge of God was born with a message from God.

Does God still speak? Yes. Can we differentiate His voice from our own subconscious? Yes. Should we ask Him questions? Yes. Does He speak audibly? Sometimes. But He may also speak by impressing your mind with words that are not heard audibly but understood unmistakably.

Will He speak to me? Ask Him to do so. Seek, and you will find. You may not hear today. Or tomorrow. But, as the Scripture promises, if you seek His wisdom, He will reply.

Can Satan speak to me? Yes. That's why it's especially important, when you think you have received a word from the Lord, to test it by the

Scriptures, measure it by the peace it brings, discuss it with other members of the Body of Christ and pray that the Lord will protect you from error.

Listen for the Lord to call you by name and reassure you of His love. Hear His voice in this way first. "Samuel. Samuel." "Jim. I love you." "Suzanne, do not be afraid." "Mary." And then, at the Garden Tomb, she knew Him.

Be encouraged.

Question 4

The Irreversible Gift?

"Can I lose my salvation? Is it possible to be saved once and then be lost again?"

This is a question often asked and a question with which we, as Christians, often wrestle. If I give my life to Jesus and embrace Him as both Savior and Lord, confessing my sin and repenting of it, is it possible for me at some later date to lose my salvation? Is it possible to receive the Lord's favor and then throw it away again? Or, put another way, once clothed by the grace of God, am I eternally secure, unable ever again to be condemned?

Eternal security is a phrase used to describe a train of thought that emphasizes the sovereign ability of God to keep those He redeems secure in His love, without regard to their post-redemptive experiences or choices. At our end of the equation, the practical effect is to emphasize the power of a single choice to accept God's gift of eternal life in Christ once and for all, irrevocably. Once I become a child of God, I will remain one by Heaven's measure, come what may, do as I will. Once saved, always saved, eternally secure, inevitably destined for glory, safe from Hell's siren call forever. This Gospel frame is also described sometimes as the perseverance of the Saints: All of those born again into God's Kingdom are saints; all saints will triumph in the end. It's a theology well-grounded in Scripture and held fast by many of the Lord's brightest and best.

It is not where I have landed, however, as I have wrestled with God's Word. That said, let me underscore my respect for all those who see Scripture as authoritative and honor it as the transcendent plumb line of theological truth. The Bible can be interpreted diversely. How I read a verse may be different from how my brother reads a verse. Both of us are seeking truth, but—seeing as through a glass darkly—each of us may have a smudge on our lenses here or there, leading us to competing conclusions. God knows our hearts and will, someday, bring us all to dazzling clarity. It's my guess that we'll all then be humbled by our errors and astonished by the breadth and depth of meaning we missed.

I value views within the Body of Christ that differ from my own on questions of this kind—questions that are not so clearly delineated in Scripture as to make argument irrefutable. I will present my outcomes and how I reason from Scripture. As I do, you must know that there are other points of view, thoughtfully drawn, with compelling rationales as well. I respect those.

This is what I think.

The question is framed by a few key biblical texts that address God's power to save from sin and its ultimate consequence and the premise that this salvation is a gift.

> **John 10:27**
> *"My sheep hear my voice, and I know them, and they follow me. I give them eternal life, and they will never perish, and no one will snatch them out of my hand. My Father, who has given them to me, is greater than all, and no one is able to snatch them out of the Father's hand. I and the Father are one."*

Jesus speaks here about His people; He speaks about people who follow Him—and that following hinges on a choice they make to follow. He emphasizes the gift of eternal life, noting that it is a gift (not earned or otherwise procured). He suggests that not only is eternal life a gift but also that it is His gift to give. His followers are eligible, by His choice, for this gift, and once received, they will not perish. No one can remove (snatch) them from the Father's hand—Jesus's hand: He and the Father are one. Jesus explains that God the Father has given these followers to Jesus the Son and no one, no thing, is more powerful than He. God the Father is Supreme; His power towers over the cosmos.

The enemy of our souls is a powerful force, too, working against us. Never underestimate his power. He is a powerful force, but His power is not greater than our God's. In this text, Jesus cites the supremacy of God in the contest for souls, the supremacy of God in the contest with Satan and the way in which Heaven will ultimately prevail. In the contest with Hell, when Christ gives eternal life to His own, Jesus claims unequivocally that hell is powerless to compromise the Lord's favor. It is a gift. Safe and secure. It is a gift that others cannot rob, steal, damage or destroy.

Ephesians 2:8-9
"God saved you by his grace when you believed. And you can't take credit for this; it is a gift from God. Salvation is not a reward for the good things we have done, so none of us can boast about it."

We must never forget that our redemption, our salvation, our promise of eternal life is a gift. It's not earned because we are better than our neighbors. It is not earned because you play by the rules or are more generous or more kind or more thoughtful or more forgiving than somebody else. It is not received because you or I somehow live above the moral norms and have maneuvered into the sight of Heaven. None of us—not one of us—nobody—can ever be good enough to earn (be entitled by our own merits or have just cause to demand) God's favor. When we understand that salvation is a gift, we can best understand these verses.

Jesus chooses to give His children, His followers, the undeserved gift of eternal life. And, as quoted by John (above), Jesus is clear: No one can take that gift away from us.

Is affirming these truths the same as saying that I cannot renounce the gift of eternal life? Or that I do not have the capacity to cast it away and walk away from my inheritance as a child of God? If I ever in my life follow Christ, do I still have an independent will enough to say (albeit foolishly and outrageously) to God, "I was once glad to receive the gift, but, honestly I don't want it anymore. I'd rather pursue my own course come what may and cease following Jesus?"

Somebody gave me a box of See's candy recently: a one-pound box. See's is a candy company born in California and well established up and down the West Coast. I like chocolate and I like See's. A lot. There are many outstanding chocolatiers in the world, of course (I know them well). Godiva.

Lindt. Good's Chocolate is a local favorite in central Indiana where I now live. But See's tastes like home to me. It reminds me of my childhood. It arouses my chocolate passions; it makes my blood run hot. Dark chocolate covered dark chocolate butter creams. My hands tremble even as I type the name. Nuts . . . and chews . . . Truffles . . . Soft centers . . . but I digress.

A friend, returning to Indiana from an excursion in the Pacific Northwest, brought me a one-pound box of See's. And I confess, without excuse or context: I received the box by his hand at 5:00 P.M. on Friday; by Saturday noon, I had consumed the whole. And I mean, the whole box. By myself. One pound. Decadent and depraved was I. Desperate. Wretched.

Having been given the box, I promise you that if you tried to take that gift away from me, I would have fought you to the last. I would have held it in my hands, clutched it to my breast, wielded my best punch in defense of my right to possess it. You would never have been able to enjoy a single bite, because I would have taken the box to my grave, clutching it in my dead, lifeless arms. You would not have it; it was a gift given to me. Mine. Not yours. Ask my family.

Having received the gift—a gift I did not purchase, did not deserve, and probably (given its artery clogging, vein busting properties) should not have had in the first place—have I surrendered my right to later throw the box away? Could I have eaten half the box and said, "Well, I don't want the other half. I'm tired of this chocolate. It satisfied my appetite for a while, but I want to explore other things now. Maybe I'll focus my passions on sushi instead for the remainder of my days?"

It's unlikely, but hypothetically, I could switch to sushi. It wouldn't make any sense (raw fish verses See's chocolate?). Such an outcome seems to me, given my experience with See's (and sushi—very unpleasant), absurd.

Once you receive a gift, do these kinds of passages suggest that you lose the ability to betray the gift in this still broken world? Nobody else can take the gift of eternal life away from me, once received from the Lord's hand—I altogether own this truth. But, can I lay it to the side?

That's the question.

Philippians 1:6
"And I am certain that God, who began the good work within you, will continue his work until it is finally finished on the day when Christ Jesus returns."

I was introduced to this verse as a student at Seattle Pacific University many years ago. It remains one of my favorite texts; it is the promise, quite literally, of a lifetime. It reminds me of God's primary role in my reformation, in my redemption. God began the work. I am not a follower of Jesus because I was sage enough or courageous enough or forward-thinking enough to choose Christ. I was prompted by God; God stirred in my heart. He knocked on the door. He presented Himself on the porch of my heart. He whispered into the deepest reach of my soul and invited me to be different. To follow Jesus. To allow Him to recreate me. And to accept the gift of eternal life. Without the Lord's intervention in our natural course, we would not even consider the higher order of Heaven, our spiritual promise or the prospect of adoption into His own family. We are, without His initiative, in my view, soulfully deaf and numb.

He begins the work. And He who begins it, will perfect it. He is going to continue prompting, working, refining and perfecting us until Christ returns, as long as our lives in this world shall last.

It is fair to consider this verse as proof of this truth: when God starts something, He finishes it. He does not fail; He does not give up; He does not surrender His purpose or plans. He does not begin working, get His hands dirty, grow frustrated and then later say to Himself, "I'm through; I guess I was wrong about that one; I guess I can't get it done, after all."

God does not start cleaning the garage and then later decide He's too tired to finish the job. When He starts a good work in you, He's not going to throw His hands up in the air and groan, "I'm through; I'm not working with you any longer; you are a loser; you are lost. Period." That is not the God disclosed in Christ or in Scripture.

I understand Philippians 1:6 in this way. If God's will is the only will in play, I will be made perfect.

But again, is affirming this truth the same as saying that He who began the good work in me is also compelling me to be perfected? Is the underlying premise of Philippians 1:6 a reality in which, once God begins to work for the good in me, my free will is eviscerated and I, without further volitional choice, will be made perfect?

I don't think so. My experience has been otherwise. And there are some other verses that require another lens of interpretation. One is called the parable of the sower. Actually, it might better be labeled the parable of the soils. It is an unforgettable teaching of Jesus in which he describes the Kingdom of God.

Luke 8:5-8
"A farmer went out to plant his seed. As He scattered it across his field, some seed fell on a footpath, where it was stepped on, and the birds ate it. Other seed fell among rocks. It began to grow, but the plant soon wilted and died for lack of moisture. Other seed fell among thorns that grew up with it and choked out the tender plants. Still other seed fell on fertile soil. This seed grew and produced a crop that was a hundred times as much as had been planted!"

After telling this story, the disciples are perplexed; they just don't get it. In direct reply to their pleas for further explanation, Jesus carefully outlines the truths captured in the illustration. He says, in part:

Luke 8:13
"The seeds on the rocky soil represent those who hear the message and receive it with joy. But since they don't have deep roots, they believe for a while, then they fall away when they face temptation."

Jesus describes a scenario in which we have the capacity to receive, with joy, the good news of the Kingdom. He explains that we can celebrate it. Embrace it. Receive it. I believe He is suggesting that we can even, as rocky soil, become believers, following the Good Shepherd. But for some reason unexplained, the root of faith is inadequate in some people; the roots are unable to sustain a living faith, especially in the face of temptations and the devil's mischief that must surely come. Clearly, there are some who, having received the seed of the Kingdom—in whom the good work is begun—fall by the wayside and are lost. Remember, the Scripture introduces us to this story as a parable of the Kingdom—an illustration of Kingdom realities.

Hebrews 3:14
"For if we are faithful to the end, trusting God just as firmly as when we first believed, we will share in all that belongs to Christ."

This passage encourages us to remain faithful. It is a text written to believers. It reminds us that our love for Jesus needs to be at the end as it was in the beginning. It's a verse that warns us against finishing the journey with less than we started with. Furthermore, it cautions us with an ***if***: ***if*** we are faithful to the end. That's a pretty big ***if***. That ***if*** is the contingent condition that determines whether or not we will **share in all that belongs to Christ**. This verse tells me I can—but may not—find myself sharing all that belongs to Christ in **the end**.

Revelation 2:4-5
"But I have this complaint against you. You don't love me or each other as you did at first! Look how far you have fallen! Turn back to me and do the works you did at first. If you don't repent, I will come and remove your lampstand from its place among the churches."

Revelation 3:15-16
"I know all the things you do, that you are neither hot nor cold. I wish that you were one or the other! But since you are like lukewarm water, neither hot nor cold, I will spit you out of my mouth!"

Ouch. Jesus is speaking to two different churches in Asia about their failures and their fall from His favor. First, the church at Ephesus does not love God as it did at first. Second, the church at Laodicea is neither hot nor cold; it lives on the fence, unwilling to commit completely, as presumably the church did when the good work began. In both cases, our Lord, with sobering certainty, declares that the churches (the believers) will be rejected—illustrated in one case by the removal of its lampstand, in the other by being spit (or in some translations, vomited) out. These dread outcomes appear to be at odds with a sense that the two congregations (and their members) have eternally secure positions in God's sovereign grace.

In these judgments I read that the condition of our hearts and the eternal consequences that follow can be altered, even after we are saved.

John 15:5-6
"Yes, I am the vine; you are the branches. Those who remain in me, and I in them, will produce much fruit. For apart from me you can do nothing. Anyone who does not remain in me is thrown away like a useless branch and withers. Such branches are gathered into a pile to be burned."

This is another "ouch" reminder. Jesus, on the night before He died, is speaking to His disciples. He is not speaking to a diverse crowd or even a church group; He is speaking to His closest friends—the men He chose, those in whom He had begun the good work. These are words of hope, power and caution. He gives them hope of becoming men of influence, bearing not just some, but much, fruit. He tells them that He will be the ongoing source of their power to become and to be. And He warns them: You can be a branch attached to My vine, but if you are not careful to *remain in Me*, you will be cut off, thrown away, burned. You can be connected to Jesus; you can also be later cut off from Him (apparently by the vintner Himself).

The separation and burning is the result of failure to produce. That failure to produce is the result of falling away from the Vine, the source of life and power. It is the result of a heart waxed cold, a soul distanced from the Spirit of Jesus that once animated and directed its course. It happens when we abandon our first love. It ends with the final break, the chopping off, the gathering to be burned.

Again, this is a New Testament record that does not persuade me that once a part of the Vine, always a part of the Vine—once saved, always saved.

> **Hebrews 6:4-6**
> *"For it is impossible to bring back to repentance those who were once enlightened – those who have experienced the good things of heaven and shared in the Holy Spirit, who have tasted the goodness of the word of God and the power of the age to come – and who then turn away from God. It is impossible to bring such people back to repentance; by rejecting the Son of God, they themselves are nailing him to the cross once again and holding him up to public shame."*

The author of this letter, writing to first-century Hebrews in Christ and to all those who have subsequently been redeemed, speaks about how some people start the journey but do not finish it. There are people who have both seen and tasted the power of the Holy Spirit in Christ and still, in time, turn away from God.

The text describes someone who, having embraced Jesus, turns his back on Jesus, walking away from Him by design. The text describes how tough—indeed, *impossible*—it is to bring someone like this back to *repentance*. The text contends that this turning away is tantamount to *rejecting the Son of God* (in the same way those who crucified Him did at Golgotha). There is no salvation without Christ; to reject Christ is to reject salvation. This is taught uniformly throughout the New Testament.

This Hebrews passage seems to me to be a bald declaration: You can repent and taste the good things of God; you can also walk away from them and stand with those who reject Christ. There is no salvation for those who reject Him. He is the Way.

> **2 Peter 2:20-21**
> *"And when people escape from the wickedness of the world by knowing our Lord and Savior Jesus Christ and then get tangled up and enslaved by sin again, they are worse off than before. It would be better if they had never known the way to righteousness than to know it and then reject the command they were given to live a holy life."*

This text is especially startling because it declares we are worse off after coming to the faith and then abandoning it, then we would have been had we never known the Savior in the first place. If delivered from sin and then returning to it, we will find ourselves in an even more desperate situation than before.

There are some who marry believing that, even though they hope to remain married for a lifetime, they may find themselves divorced, and that, if later divorced, they will somehow be restored to the singleness they knew before their marriage. Sadly, marriages do unravel and people do get divorced.

But once you stand forward to marry, exchange vows, and pledge your life to another, you do so with Heaven as a witness (church ceremony or not). Once that happens, your life is changed forever. You may later divorce and find yourself single again. But you can never be restored to the same place you were before you were married. Life just does not work that way. You may pick up the pieces and move on, but nothing is ever the same. Two do not become one and then become two again without being changed.

In a way, professing Christ carries the same promise. When you proclaim your faith in Christ by being baptized, for instance, you stand forward and make a public declaration of the intention of your heart, your commitment for a lifetime. All of Heaven—and yes, I believe, hell, too—watches. Baptism is the penultimate testimony of intention; the washing of sin away, the old self dead and buried, the raising to new life in Christ, repentance, the new birth of our soul—all are captured in the testimonial of baptism. We say, essentially, "I do," in response to the question of the ages: Do you take this One to be your Savior, your Lord, your all?

And then we walk forward into a new day.

Sadly, as in many marriages, one of the partners eventually grows weary, for whatever reason, of the relationship, of the arrangement, of the commitment. In the case of a relationship with Jesus, He is never the one who strays; He is faithful; He will work to make the relationship perfect to the last. We, on the other hand, can be weak and selfish, blind.

You profess your love—even being baptized—and then you conclude that the relationship is just not worth the effort it requires. You want to be single again, making your own way through life without always having to think about Him. Perhaps the soil of your heart is rocky; the roots of love do not grow deep enough.

Whatever the reason, you may walk away. And when you do, you are not restored to the way things were before you gave yourself to Jesus. Life doesn't work that way. You are changed. Forever. Walking away, you will not find the place you were before you were a believer. You will be worse off than you were before.

You don't just walk away from Jesus. You slap Him. You nail Him to the tree once more. You hold Him up to ridicule. You've moved from the thief on the cross who humbly sought to honor Jesus to the thief who cursed Him.

All of this suggests that it's possible to be saved and then to throw your salvation away. It cannot be taken from you; only you can discard it. Nothing can separate you from the love of Christ . . .except your will.

Look at the words of Jesus as He tells a parable about the end of the age. In all of the Lord's teaching about the end of this world, there is a universal thread: When the end comes, you must be ready. No one knows when the end will come, no one knows when Jesus will return, but when He does, be ready. The emphasis is on vigilance: stay alert, do not become lackadaisical, be focused. It is not enough to be ready today, relax and forget about it, imagining that if the end comes fifty years from now, your preparation today will have been enough. No, as long as life shall last, be careful with the talents given, be certain you remain attached to the Vine, beware of the devil "who prowls about like a roaring lion, looking for someone to devour" (1 Peter 5:8). You must invest in your faith for a lifetime, to be ready.

> **Matthew 24:45-51**
> *"A faithful, sensible servant is one to whom the master can give the responsibility of managing his other household servants and feeding them. If the master returns and finds that the servant has done a good job, there will be a reward. I tell you the truth, the master will put that servant in charge of all he owns. But what if the servant is evil and thinks, 'My master won't be back for awhile,' and he begins beating the other servants, partying, and getting drunk? The master will return unannounced and unexpected, and he will cut the servant to pieces and assign him a place with the hypocrites. In that place there will be weeping and gnashing of teeth."*

This is not the smiling Jesus we prefer on the cover of our Bible storybooks. This vision of Jesus returning and dismembering the unfaithful servant and tossing him into the company of the doomed challenges us. It's a troubling tale, of course, but Jesus comprehends the terror of hell. He is not content for anyone to be blithely en route there. He comprehends the reality of justice; He knows there is a consequence for every wrong done; He died to balance the scale of justice, so that we might escape what we have earned by our sin. This parable reminds us that even the Lord's servants can lose touch with their privileged status and squander their inheritance, finding themselves outside of grace. The master's servant in this story succumbs to evil and is placed with the hypocrites—those who pretend to be what they are not.

Remember, we are warned—we who are believers are warned—to watch out for the devil who seeks to devour. If we could not be devoured, we would not need to be warned.

Choosing to become a Christ follower—to be born again—allows us to receive the free gift of eternal life. It does not preclude the possibility of choosing to fall away.

> **1 John 2:1-6**
> *"My dear children, I am writing this to you so that you will not sin. But if anyone does sin, we have an advocate who pleads our case before the Father. He is Jesus Christ, the one who is truly righteous.*

> *He himself is the sacrifice that atones for our sins – and not only our sins but the sins of all the world.*
>
> *"And we can be sure that we know him if we obey his commandments. If someone claims, 'I know God,' but doesn't obey God's commandments, that person is a liar and is not living in the truth. But those who obey God's word truly show how completely they love him. That is how we know we are living in him. Those who say they live in God should live their lives as Jesus did."*

It is the intention of God that we be redeemed and be made perfect. We are not to simply understand that Jesus died on our behalf on the cross and then continue living as we did before. No, we are to repent (turn away from the old path and pursue a new one). We are to be born again, empowered to write our biographies on a fresh, clean page.

We are not perfect. I have never met anyone who was without flaw. I've met some who've imagined themselves to be perfect, but I have never met anyone who was married to one of them. This is not to say we are doomed; it is to say we must confess our sin, our imperfection, before we can be made new.

The book of 1 John was written, it says, so that we can know that we are saved. We should have certainty of our salvation. He to whom we confess is just. He will forgive us our sins when we admit them. If, later, anyone does sin, we have an Advocate who pleads before the Father. Jesus is at the bar of Heaven speaking for you, arguing your case in the face of the devil's accusations. He is qualified to do so because He is the Christ.

Can I, then, go on with my life here below, in sin and disobedience, because I have Jesus as my defense above? John would not agree. Those who love God prove their love by the way they obey His word.

The question of eternal security may not be as important as the question of assurance, the security of knowing you are saved.

If I believe my salvation cannot be lost, sin calls into question the validity of my salvation. If I am really saved, why am I failing in my Christian walk? Alternately, if I believe my salvation can be lost, sin also calls into question my salvation. If I sin, I am lost.

The question then for all of us is this: Can we live up to the high and holy calling of God? Can we be empowered by His Holy Spirit to live in better ways than we lived before we were saved? Once saved, can I stare down temptations that otherwise would have wrecked me?

When redeemed by Christ and filled by His Spirit, temptations once irresistible can become resistible. Refuse to resist them—refuse to repent—and you will find yourself cycling in sin in the same dysfunctional way as before. Your spiritual life will be maimed, your spiritual power emaciated, and your relationship with God distant, at best. Whether you believe in eternal security or not, the outcome will be the same in this life. You will be a shadow of what might have been, uncertain of life in this world and the world to come.

However, when your heart is dedicated to pleasing the One who bought you with His own blood and that dedication is focused on resisting the devil who seeks only your harm, peace and assurance of God's favor begin to clothe and cover you. This peace can become a constant, even if you stumble here and there. God knows your heart and your heart's ambition.

What we consider to be sin must be the subject of another discussion. Sometimes, people are haunted and stalked by things that by the Bible does not define as sin. Sometimes, we are troubled by the devil's whisper that we are not ever good enough.

Jesus paid the price for your sin.

No matter what you've done—no matter what your failure—He has paid for it. But you must choose to walk away from it. You cannot choose to continue to live in the repeating cycle of that from which He died to save you and expect eternal security.

When my mother was a child, she and her sister wanted to go to a theatre to see a movie. In the church world in which she was raised, movies were forbidden, thought to be emblems of a corrupt world. This was not uncommon in the holiness tradition of the early 20th century. Of course, her family's prohibition against motion pictures was quite countercultural; movies were very popular everywhere else.

One day, at age ten or eleven, my mom hatched a plan with her sister Marguerite to see a movie.[1] They went to my grandmother's pantry, climbed up the shelves, pulled down some jars of homemade pickles, pulled on their coats and ran out of the house without permission or notice.

They ran down the steep street on which their house stood, flying down the hill to the center of Fremont, a Seattle neighborhood that had a theatre. They sold the pickles to a man walking by, took the money immediately to the ticket window and soon found themselves huddled in two theatre seats. With eyes big as saucers, the two young girls were quickly drawn into a black-and-white drama on the big screen, in which a young girl about their age was kidnapped. My mother does not remember the name of the picture, who starred in the story or even what happened next in the movie.

What she remembers is the sheer terror she and her sister felt in the theatre, imagining that Jesus would return at any moment, and they would both be surely condemned to a lake of burning fire. They tried to focus on the film but could see only Satan's horns and a pitchfork in their mind's eye until, unable to bear the fear no longer, they jumped from their seats and ran back into the broad light of day outside.

My mother still wonders, in the back of her mind, what happened to the little girl kidnapped on the silver screen. Was she reunited with her family? Were the bad guys apprehended? Did the little girl live happily ever after? We'll never know. Although it's probably safe to say that an afternoon matinee in 1931 had a happy ending.

My mother's childhood trauma-at-the-movies story illustrates the point that we are too often intimidated by things that are very unlikely to send us to hell. There is nothing in Scripture to support the notion that God will seize little children who go to movies and cast them into perdition for it. The devil is forever in the business of undermining our faith, attempting to persuade us that we are lost anyway and should just give up.

It is possible to lose your salvation, though it may not be as easy as you have been taught to believe. But it can be done, and you need to align your heart with Christ.

If today there is some master in your life who is greater than Jesus, then you're in a danger zone. Your salvation is in play. If there's another master who is calling you and leading you and compelling you to do things that you know are not right, then you need to be aware that, previous professions notwithstanding, eternity can hang in the balance.

Perhaps you're involved in a sexual relationship that you know is not right, for instance. Maybe you are trafficking in awful gossip that wounds others and does not build others up. Or you've been sidetracked by greed and materialism. Perhaps drunkenness is a problem.

These are listed repeatedly in the New Testament as things that will deny you access to the Kingdom of God. If you are serving a master who is calling you into these kinds of things, then Jesus is not your master and your salvation is in jeopardy.

But be encouraged: He is willing to be restored to the throne of your heart and to restore your eternal security. He's willing to take you back. The choice is yours. Confess your sin, decide to come clean and walk fresh. Let Jesus make things right once more.

All of us would do well to ask Him to search us and disclose if there is anything in our hearts that displeases Him. He will always honor our quest to have more of His mind and Spirit.

The devil will not rest. Neither will our God. The contest for our souls is ongoing and real. But Jesus will surely prevail in us, if we let Him. If we hold on to Him. If we remain with Him. Place your hand in His and don't let go. You will then be saved. You can be sure of it.

Qustion 3

Christianity Compared

"How would you compare Christianity to other world religions? What are the similarities and differences between Christians and Muslims, Hindus, Mormons, Jehovah Witnesses, Jews, Buddhists, etc.?"

This question presumes that some things are similar in all of these faith systems and some things differentiate them, setting them apart. This is, of course, absolutely true.

It's also true that we could easily read several volumes on each of these ways of looking at the world and attend a week-long conference and not exhaust the subject. To address the expanse and depth of each faith is the stuff of lifetimes.

Still, it is possible to appropriately thumbnail some of the basic premises undergirding each, in a comparative way, while acknowledging that this chapter cannot be a comprehensive tutorial in any of them. I will answer the question through the lens of Christianity, noting how devotion to Christ especially makes a difference in the comparison. Mine will admittedly be a biased analysis, reflecting on non-Christian thought from a Christian point-of-view; some may conclude the answer given is neither balanced nor fair. Nevertheless, I will attempt to share my understanding respectfully and honestly, knowing that all of us necessarily approach comparative challenges of this kind with a kind of experiential and intellectual screen. My screen happens to be a Christian one.[1]

That said, let's identify some of the similarities that bring all of these faith-based worldviews into focus. The Bible's book of beginnings is a good place to start:

Genesis 1:1
"In the beginning God created the heavens and the earth."

Few phrases in all of literature are more famous than this one. In this astounding assertion, found in text held sacred by both Christians and Jews, a foundational truth is proclaimed. There is a beginning. Furthermore, God was at the beginning and before the beginning. He is the creator and author of the material order we now know. He is the intelligent and personal catalyst of things seen and unseen. This platform, with a few variations, is at the core of almost all systems of faith and religious thought. It is an important starting place, because it is where we all have to start when making decisions about what we believe and do not believe. We must all, sooner or later, come to terms with the creation story, don't we? True or false: Is there a creator or is the universe the product of blind and random forces operating without design? We all have to eventually come to terms with the question: Does God exist?

Only two options are open to us when wrestling with the origin of things. First, after exploring the world around us, attempting to understand how it works and why, we might conclude that there is no God—that the order we observe in nature has been born by random forces working by chance, each edging the other, acting and reacting blindly. Second, we might conclude that the order we observe in nature is the product of intelligent design, orchestrated by an infinite Divine that at some level exists apart from, even as He (it?) is reflected in what can, under this head, be called *creation*. These are the options; door number one or door number two. Each of us must choose one or the other.

I am persuaded that the Genesis principle ("In the beginning, God . . .") is the most sensible. It appeals to my sense of logic. I have been dubbed emotional, intuitive and, by some (and not always kindly), even mystical; all accurately capture some part of me. But at my core, I think myself grounded fundamentally in native logic. That is the way I seemed to be wired. As I survey the world around me, it seems eminently more plausible to believe in God than it does in chance as the author of a physical universe so precisely tuned as to allow journeys to the moon or exploration of DNA. Disciplines of knowledge like mathematics, physics and medicine all argue, from my point of view, for intelligent design. Fixed laws in the hard sciences, for instance, beg for a lawgiver.

Science never invents new knowledge; it can only discover preexisting truth. A scientific advance is a scientific discovery. We can discover only what already exists. In this sense, both science and theology grapple with transcendent eternal realities. All knowledge does. Sounds like God-talk to me.

How is it that plants grow, that seeds encapsulate life, that flowers bloom, that salmon travel the world and find their way back to their place of origin, that our bodies move, that our eyes see, that music exists or that the moon and planets move with mathematical precision? All of these and more beg for an overarching design, an engineer, an artist, a creator, a supernatural being, a God.

The pursuit of science, which some imagine to be an alternative faith, assumes that there are immutable laws and fixed outcomes that can be uncovered and understood. To me, the laws themselves suggest a lawgiver.

It seems altogether rational to me to believe that there is a God before the beginning, a creator of all things, an intelligent catalyst that launched the world and its timeline. It's a logical, intellectual step to take, not just for me but for most of the major religions on this list. That there is an originator, a God, a personal being at work in the beginning is widely held. Christians believe that. Muslims believe that. Mormons believe that. Jehovah's Witnesses believe that. Jews believe that.

Hindus and Buddhists have a somewhat different take on the supernatural origin of things; they see the world quite differently from the monotheistic systems of thought arising from the Jewish concept of a personal God. These Asian religions do not comprehend a single personal God bringing an ordered world to life in the same way as the others do.

It's important to know that Buddhism is a descendant of Hinduism. The Buddha himself was a Hindu prince who, in a way, launched a reform of the more ancient Hinduism practiced in his lifetime. The two religions are closely connected, even if they now have evolved into distinct religious philosophies.

Hinduism sees an impersonal, transcendent life force sustaining the universe. It is an impersonal power that is difficult for humanity (especially those of us nurtured in Western thought) to grasp or understand. It's a life force that does not necessarily have a name, although it can be referred to as *karma*. It exists as a state of being, a great oneness. The word nirvana was popularized in our culture in the 1990s by Kurt Cobain and his band, born in the Seattle grunge scene. It is a word taken from Hindu and Buddhist theology, referring to the ultimate release of the soul into the ultimate oneness of this pervasive life force. To be released into Nirvana is to be made free from the struggles and challenges of life as we know it.

Hindu scriptures—the Hindu Vedas—record stories of the gods, including stories of one Brahmin deity considered to be the creator god. But even this narrative is part of a larger collection of god stories, one in a pantheon—a family—of gods, all of which are subordinate to the larger karma. This polytheistic foundation separates Hindu and Buddhist thought from the other primary world religions; all the rest affirm the power of a creator that can be known and named in a personal, interactive way.

Jehovah's Witnesses and, especially, Mormons sometimes chafe at being listed separately from Christians, as if they are not Christians. Jehovah's Witnesses recognize Jesus, but focus on the God expressed in the name Jehovah (a name derived from the addition of vowels to the line-up of Hebrew consonants in the Old Testament: YHWH, a name for God thought so sacred that the vowels were dropped in antiquity and lost). The Witnesses are little concerned with being labeled Christians or not. Mormons, on the other hand, see themselves as Christians and want to be called Christian. Their official church name is the Church of Jesus Christ of Latter Day Saints (LDS). The moniker *Mormon* comes from the *Book of Mormon*, which tells the story of ancient peoples in the new world of the Americas; the book is thought to have been supernaturally delivered to their prophet Joseph Smith in the 19th century by the angel Moroni. Mormons line this book up alongside the Bible; no one else does. Mormons emphasize their Christian roots these days, however. Perhaps you've noticed how the name, *Church of Jesus Christ*, has been moved to the fore of their presentation of themselves in recent years.

Both the Witnesses and the Mormons, although radically different from one another, hold views that are very different, at their core, from what can be described as *orthodox* Christianity. The word orthodox in this context is descended from an ancient Greek pairing of words meaning "right thinking" or "right doing." This use of the word transcends denominational labels like Catholicism, Orthodox churches, Protestantism. Each of these three branches of Christianity hold anchors in common—anchors that the Witnesses and Mormons do not share. It is fair to think of them separately, apart from orthodox Christianity.

But adherents in all of these systems of thought—Christians, Jews, Jehovah's Witnesses, Mormons, and Muslims—understand there to be a personal, creator God. *In the beginning God.* They would all embrace this idea in a way that Hindus and Buddhists would not; Hindus and Buddhists acknowledge the supremacy of the spiritual order over the material one, but do not recognize a single personal, creator God in the same way.

This then, reflects one similarity and one difference at the base of each religion.

Matthew 7:12
"Do to others whatever you would like them to do to you. This is the essence of all that is taught in the law and the prophets."

This is one of Christ's most famous quotes: the Golden Rule. Through the centuries, these words of Jesus have been compared to other teachings and other systems of thought to argue that they are equivalent with Christianity. It is a popular prop for the premise, "All religions share a common ethic and morality. It doesn't, in the end, really matter which path you take to Heaven. We're all going to the same destination and along the way on this journey, this concept of treating others the way you want to be treated is fundamental to all faith systems, a universally held truth."

Jesus expressed this idea most completely and in active terms. There are other faiths that claim similar wisdom, but it is never expressed with the same force and clarity. Jesus compels us to act; others take a more passive approach.

In some Asian faiths for instance, the maxim reads: "Do not do anything to someone else that you do not want them to do to you." This frames the principle in the negative. It proclaims a more passive, more reactive course: When making a decision about what to do, "don't do something you don't want to have done." This is quite a bit different from the counsel of Jesus: "I want you to take the initiative to bless someone else—do good for them—in the same way you would like them to bless and do good for you." Reach out to someone else in the way that you would like someone else to reach out to you. That's proactive, compelling, inspiring.

Perhaps my analysis is hair-splitting on this point. In the end, there is a commonly held theme in world religions; there is a sense of reciprocity in all of these moral codes. Much religious thought across a broad spectrum has its root in the Old Testament, which first introduced the Golden Rule (see Leviticus 19:17-18). Jesus restated this Old Testament truth in a way easy to understand and grasp. It is an ancient idea that surfaced long before Jesus walked in this world.

Again, looking at our list—Christians, Mormons, Jews, Jehovah's Witnesses, Muslims—all have this common theological root first developed in the Old Testament, owning in one way or another this Golden Rule. Hindus and Buddhists do not embrace this idea in the same way. This is not to say they do not embrace a noble moral order; for them, the moral order is framed somewhat differently. Hinduism and Buddhism, for instance, elevate alms giving and generosity, too, but in a context of material self-denial. Denying the power and even reality of the material world is a traditional Hindu reference point; ascetic disciplines designed to escape material struggles define a spiritual journey in Hindu or Buddhist thought more centrally than do relationships to other people. The Golden Rule makes relationships with others a central focus. Escaping the suffering of this world into the impersonal and tranquil Nirvana is the object in Hindu and Buddhist pursuits; relating to a personal God is the object of the others.

Divorcing yourself from the painful reality of this world is a different motivator than alleviating the painful reality of someone else. You can see these emphases played out on the stage of the great civilizations fashioned over centuries by Hinduism and Buddhism. In these cultures, the development of charitable structures and systems has lagged behind those of other cultures. I am not arguing that these civilizations are in any way morally inferior, I assert only that the evolution of civilizations is greatly influenced by the religions that frame them.

In the end, this idea of the Golden Rule, although expressed in a compelling and concise way by Jesus, is not exclusive to the Christian religion, but widely held across the spectrum of faith.

Contending that there is a personal, creator God and that there are active ways in which we must relate to others for the good differentiates Western and Eastern religious traditions.

And according to these religions, what happens to us as we come to life's close?

Hebrews 9:27-28
"And just as each person is destined to die once and after that comes judgment, so also Christ died once for all time as a sacrifice to take away the sins of many people. He will come again, not to deal with our sins, but to bring salvation to all who are eagerly waiting for him."

All of us are going to die once, and when we die, then comes the judgment. In some way, our lives in this world set the stage for the moment we die. When we die, there will be an evaluation, a calculation. Then there will be an administration of justice for each us, a sentencing hinged on the choices made in this life. This concept is broadly held and woven into many religions. Every religion acknowledges death and argues for an afterlife. Where religions differ is not in the fact of death but in what happens next.

Does the judgment come next? Almost everyone in these major religions believes it does. In all the different faith systems, you'll recognize this pattern of death followed by the judgment. Christians believe they will die and then comes the judgment. Muslims believe it. Mormons believe it. Jehovah Witnesses and Jews believe it, too.

Hindus and Buddhists, again, do not see things in the same way. They believe they will die and then face, not a judgment so much as a retooling for life ongoing. This is where the concept of reincarnation comes into play. Reincarnation suggests that once dead, you are spun back into this world again. How you re-enter and in what form is a reflection of how you have lived in your life (lives). With each cycle of life—each reincarnation—you hope to live in such a way as to spin out of this cycle into the Nirvana. There is an element of karmic justice in this process, to be sure, but it is not equivalent to personal judgment at the bar of a personal, albeit divine, judge.

Hindus and Buddhists have well developed understandings of sin and failure. They comprehend guilt and shame as do those in other faith systems. They believe that how each of us lives in the here and now has a profound impact on how we will live in the hereafter. But in their view, sin does not lead to a point of judgment so much as it encumbers and delays progress toward Nirvana in prolonged life cycles of reincarnation.

This is why you find Hindus bathing in the sacred River Ganges, for instance, just as the sun comes up across the water at Varanasi at the break of day. This ritual bath is thought to help expedite the journey to Nirvana and wash away sin. There are other rituals to the same end in Hindu thought; but all underscore the different understanding of life and death in an Asian frame of reference from that understood in the monotheistic religions born in the Middle East.

If we are to be judged, what will happen? How will we be judged?

> **Ephesians 2:8-10**
> *"God saved you by his grace when you believed. And you can't take credit for this; it is a gift from God. Salvation is not a reward for the good things we have done, so none of us can boast about it. For we are God's masterpiece. He has created us anew in Christ Jesus, so we can do the good things he planned for us long ago."*

This is where Christianity stands alone. This text tells us that when we find ourselves, after death, at the day of reckoning, we can be saved from the consequences of our own failure, our sin, but not because of how we balanced the scales of justice by doing good. If we are able to balance the scales of justice by doing good, effectively neutralizing the weight of our bad, then it could be said that we earned our redemption. At the judgment, then, we would deserve and could fairly demand acquittal.

However, this seminal passage from Ephesians reminds us that the only way we can escape condemnation at the judgment is by the receipt of a gift—not earned, not deserved, only received. It will be a pass not purchased but given as a gift. The gift is possible because someone else paid our debt. Someone else intervened so that we might go free. Justice and the consequence of sin are still fulfilled; there is no compromise or denial of the wrongdoing; it is just that someone else has paid our dues in our stead.

This arrangement is necessary because, through the lens of the New Testament, not one of us is competent or able to do enough good to make up for the wrong we have done. And, unless the price for our wrongdoing is satisfied, we are doomed. There is no other remedy for our guilt, our shame, our sentence.

When we say we are "saved," we acknowledge that we have been saved from the deserved consequence of our sin. This gift cannot be earned or purchased. It is a gift of grace, unmerited favor, received when we believe in the Cross of Christ and surrender into His will.

We cannot take credit for it; we cannot be proud. We cannot say, "Well, I've lived in such a way that I'm going to glory. I have earned the right to go to glory. When I get to Heaven's gate, I'll be able to explain that even though I've made some mistakes along the way, I've made up for them. I'm better than most. I've been good enough to qualify." It will not work that way. **Salvation is not a reward for the good things we have done, so none of us can boast about it.**

In other words, we can never say to God, "You owe me. You must do. . . ." God is greater than His creation. We can only receive His gift; this is uniquely Christian. Christians are the only ones who believe in the *gift* of salvation.

Muslims believe that they must earn their salvation. They believe in a just God, called in Arabic, *Allah*. In the Islamic view, the day of judgment will be hinged on the good and bad deeds of a lifetime and how they add up. If the sum of those deeds is positive, there is a reward. If it is negative—that is, if the amount and severity of negative conduct or thought is greater than the positive—there is punishment and condemnation. Islamic theology contends that there are actually two different personalities, as if an angel and a demon, fixed on everyone's shoulders; these two keep record of everything you do. Your thoughts, your conduct, your deeds, your gestures, even your silence—everything is noted; you can never really know how the ledgers will ultimately stack up. You just never know. You can work hard to do the right stuff and try your best to get the positive to outweigh the negative, but there's no clear, definitive way to know whether at the end you will be rewarded or punished. It's altogether possible that you will overlook a stray thought or incidental gesture that will negatively impact your eternal destiny because you inadvertently forgot to compensate with an extra good deed. This uncertainty makes peace of mind necessarily elusive.

That's the way of works-based righteousness; it all depends on you.

The same is true in the Mormon religion. Your eternal destiny is determined by your conduct in this life alone. Your prospects are determined not by what you believe but by what you do. Salvation is not a gift from God; it is earned by the way you perform.

Jehovah's Witnesses also embrace a performance-based redemption. Salvation is offered to those who work for and live up to the assignments, rules and regulations outlined in their understanding of God's law. Salvation is not experienced as a free gift in Christ.

Jews live for the Law; grace is understood but not determinative. In the different branches of the Jewish religion—diverse expressions ranging from the more liberally oriented Reformed to the conservative edges of the Orthodox—redemption is available to those who keep the Law and, essentially therefore, earn it. A gift given freely is not part of the equation.

Hindus, as already mentioned, believe they are in a process of matriculating, through a series of reincarnations and/or ritual disciplines, out of this world into a sublime oneness. Buddhists adhere to similar concepts, although polished in different ways over time. I have visited spectacular Buddhist temples, carved into mountainsides, in which ancient monks sat and denied themselves food and water for the purpose of advancing their cause, divorcing themselves from the realities of this world so that Nirvana would be within reach. No free gifts there, only hard work and the discipline of self-denial.

All but one of the religions, then, focus on what you can do, must do, to save yourself. The Christian faith alone, the teaching of the New Testament alone, proclaims that we have hope because of an unmerited and free gift of eternal life. The opposite side of the coin is that there is nothing we can do, there is no amount of good we can do, to make ourselves worthy; Jesus alone, is worthy.

> **1 Corinthians 15:3-4**
> *"I passed on to you what was most important and what had also been passed on to me. Christ died for our sins, just as the Scriptures said. He was buried, and he was raised from the dead on the third day, just as the Scriptures said."*

In this passage, you will find the basic platform of Christianity, four truths that separate the Christian religion from all the rest. There are four things you must never forget:

1) Who Jesus was.
2) What Jesus did.
3) The problem of sin.
4) How Jesus dealt with sin.

Jesus is the Christ (the Greek word for the *Messiah*, the chosen one of God). He is the One who came. Christ crucified. He is the One who brought upon Himself the consequence of our sin. The hope of the gospel is that Jesus stood in our place. No other religion believes that anybody else could stand in our place.

In all other systems of thought, we have to work out our redemption on our own. In the Christian gospel, Jesus stands in our place, doing what we cannot do so that we can be blessed with a gift we do not deserve. This plan of salvation is made possible by a loving, merciful, just and holy God. He satisfies the requirements of His own law by offering His own Son in our stead.

God, in the person of His son, Jesus, bore our sin and its eternal consequence, on the Cross. Christians believe that Jesus is God. This is where Christianity also diverges from groups like the Jehovah's Witnesses and Mormons. Jehovah's Witnesses and Mormons honor the Old and New Testaments, but read them differently; neither of them believes that Jesus is God in the way that orthodox Christianity does.

You may find a Mormon who says that they do believe that Jesus is the Son of God, but Mormon theology includes a doctrine called "eternal progression." Simply stated, we are part of a progression: We are what God once was, we are what Jesus once was, and we are becoming more and more like Him. As He was, we are; as He is, we will be. In Mormon theology, the Jesus that was the Son of God, who was once here on earth, is just one of many other gods on other planets. We can progress eternally (well, actually men can progress eternally) to become gods just like Jesus. When we die, if we live in the right way now, our reward will be that we will receive our own planet to govern just as Jesus came here and governed here. Then we will be Jesus for another planet. This promise is gender specific, although Mormon women also have the hope of eternal progression, it is in the shadow of their husbands. And while Jesus is, in this way, revered as a supernatural being, Mormons hold quite a different concept of Jesus than does orthodox Christianity.

Jehovah's Witnesses do not believe that Jesus was himself God. They have produced their own translation of the Bible (called the *New World Translation*), which reinterprets some passages that proclaim Christ as divine. John 1:1 (NIV), for instance, the famous, "In the beginning was the Word and the Word was with God and the Word was God." is rewritten to say, "In [the] beginning the Word was, and the Word was with God, and the Word was a god." [2] It's a simple word, "a." But it changes the whole dynamic sense and meaning; it is inserted in the text, it is not in the original manuscripts and the *New World Translation* is the only Bible translation that has it. Whatever might be said about the translation, my point here is to underscore that the Witnesses see Jesus quite differently than do Christians in the Orthodox, Catholic, and Protestant churches.

Muslims, of course, see Muhammad as the Prophet and the penultimate revealer of God's will and way. They recognize Jesus as a prophet, too, but subordinate to Muhammad—who is certainly not divine.

Hindus and Buddhists see Jesus as extraordinary, but again, only in the sense that other great teachers and spiritual voices have been extraordinary. The singular Son of a singular God is, for them, beyond the pale.

Jesus is Himself God. No other faith owns this claim. And Jesus is the atonement. He is the substitution for our sin. He's the one who took it upon Himself. There is no other faith system that argues that Jesus or anyone else has done such a thing. Christianity recognizes that sin (wrongdoing, wrong thought, wrong being, the brokenness, the imperfection, the failure to be perfect) denies us life. Sin has corrupted all of creation, including human nature. Sin separates us from God.

Christianity recognizes Jesus as the bridge back to God. He covers our sin and makes it possible for us to become perfect in Heaven's eyes, to be perfect before God, and, therefore to be in eternity with God. Jesus is the answer to the problem of sin. He is the Way, the Truth, and the Life. No other religion owns that.

Notice, at the last, the Scriptures. **We preach about Christ crucified for our sin** (see 1 Corinthians 1:23). The Old and New Testaments, the Bible, are the authoritative definition of truth in the Christian world. One thing is true whether you are an orthodox believer from the Syrian Orthodox Church, the Coptic Orthodox Church, the Romanian or Russian Orthodox Church—all of which believe they are the descendants of the first-century church—or part of the Roman Catholic church (which also believes it is descended from the first-century church), or a Protestant—part of a church family descended from those who also trace their roots to the beginning of Christianity through the reformation of ancient traditions. No matter which branch of the Christian family to which you belong, all hold a reverence for and deference to the Scripture that does not exist in the other groups.

So, what's the difference? What are the similarities?

All faith systems acknowledge the spiritual nature of life. All faith systems acknowledge that there are some broken places within our spirits that need to be mended. All systems attempt to come to terms with death.

In all systems except the Christian religion, our ability to come to terms with our imperfections, our death and our eternal future, is dependent on us and our ability to work for—to earn—God's favor and our redemption.

The gospel of Jesus, on the other hand, alone proclaims the supremacy of Christ as our Redeemer. Christians know He did for us what we cannot do. And so, as seen through the lens of Christ, all other faith systems, while well intentioned, cannot deliver, because they require us to purchase what we can never buy: God's gift of eternal life.

When sizing up the options, each of us must ask: Am I willing to stake my future on my conduct alone? Am I willing to risk everything on my ability to be good enough? Am I willing to face God on my own terms, believing that I can earn God's favor and demand His reward? Am I willing to face a holy God without an intermediary standing with me, for me?

Given these questions, would you say that your situation is hopeless? Try as you might, you cannot do it. You try to do right, but sometimes you do wrong. You have a memory of past failure that haunts and shadows you. If left to your ability alone, you know will never be good enough.

And, if that's true, then what?

Then Jesus. Because Jesus is perfect. He who knew no sin takes ours as His own. And in the covering of Jesus' blood, we can be redeemed. We can be called to be better than we are. We can be empowered to live above the sin that so easily entangles us. But it depends on Him and acceptance of His gift of life. That is the fundamental dividing line for all ages, all of humanity and all religions.

We who follow Christ are in a place that very much stands alone.

There's so much more that could be said, and the Christian religion has so much more depth than just this simple premise. There are many other things we might learn about other faith systems. Please understand that it is not my intention to diminish them except to say that they are quite different in their approach, and they are all on one side of the ledger while the followers of Jesus are on the other.

Today, know this: When you look at other systems of thought and try to measure them against one another, you can always bring Jesus to the center. He is the center. What a religion believes about Jesus, who He is and what He did, what they believe about sin being a problem and what Jesus did about it—these will be the dividing marks between Christianity and everything else.

At the last, choose the faith that elevates Jesus above all other things and you will do well. There is only one faith that does that: Christianity.

Question 2

Applying Scripture

"How can I tell the difference between passages in the Bible that should be interpreted literally (e.g., "Thou shalt not steal."), figuratively (e.g. "If your right eye offends you, cut it out."), and contextually (e.g., "Women should have long, straight hair.")? What do I do when Bible passages that have long been thought to be literal may now be seen as figurative or contextual?"

I am part of a movement within the larger Christian family called the Church of God,[1] which believes that the Bible reigns supreme in the quest to understand our Maker and His will in this world. The Bible is held to be the supernaturally revealed word of God. We do not have a formal book of discipline or doctrinal statement. We do not have a written list of do's and don'ts. We do not recognize an ancillary text that defines for us how we understand the Scripture. Historically, the Church of God has been simply devoted to the premise that the Bible is the ultimate plumb line by which we measure ideas and conduct. That is how we have seen ourselves, anyway.

In fact, however, the Church of God has a particular way of approaching the Scripture, which was born in the "holiness tradition" grounded in Wesleyan theology and culturally framed within the context of 19th-century America. The edges of this approach have been shaved over time, reinterpreted at some points on the periphery, but the essential core remains in play. The Bible is fundamental to who we are—as a church, as a family, as a congregation of Christ-followers. How we read it, how we interpret it, how we systemically understand it, will determine how we apply it and how it defines us. This is true for all those who revere the Word, whatever our theological frame. The question above speaks exactly to this issue.

How do we know what we're reading? How do we differentiate what's literal and what's figurative? How do we apply it to the here and now?

There is almost universal assent within the Christian and academic communities, across all denominational and theological lines, about what words actually appear in the most ancient biblical manuscripts. In other words, there is very little dispute about the text itself.

> **John 1:1**
> *"In the beginning the Word already existed. The Word was with God, and the Word was God. He existed in the beginning with God. God created everything through him, and nothing was created except through him."*

There is no real argument about whether or not the original Greek of the text above (from which this English translation has been made) is valid and authentic. Presbyterians, Methodists, Roman Catholics, Baptists, Lutherans, and all the rest agree that that is what it says. There is no textual dispute about the verse in Revelation 20 that declares that Jesus will reign for 1,000 years. Everyone agrees that this sentence is a part of the historic New Testament narrative.

> **Revelation 20:4**
> *"They all came to life again, and they reigned with Christ for a thousand years."*

The disagreements do not arise so much from the text itself as they do from how to interpret the agreed-upon text. The words are not in dispute; the meaning of the words sometimes is. Christians all read the same page—the same words—but often understand them differently. We can agree on the text, but what does it mean?

It can be difficult to differentiate between what content to take literally and what to understand figuratively. For instance, in the 1,000 year reign of Christ referenced above, should we understand a literal 1,000 years or does 1,000 years indicate a figurative expression of a vast span of time? Does not the Bible say elsewhere that "a day unto the Lord is like 1,000 years?" Which is it: one thousand years or an expression meaning a very long time?

How you interpret a text, obviously, can have a profound impact on where you land on a whole range of theological and practical applications.

2 Timothy 3:15-16
"All Scripture is inspired by God and is useful to teach us what is true and to make us realize what is wrong in our lives. It corrects us when we are wrong and teaches us to do what is right. God uses it to prepare and equip his people to do every good work."

This is a self-attesting verse, in which the Bible seems to authenticate itself.

These are the words of Paul written to Timothy—and, we believe, to all believers in all time. We believe they are the words of God transmitted by Paul. The Scripture, though written by many different authors in three different languages on three different continents over the period of 1,600 years, is woven together by a single thread of thought, as if the product of a single mind. From Genesis to Revelation, there is a continuity and cohesiveness, a unity of thought, pointing to the redemptive plan of God, which requires the acknowledgment of one Author. This particular Scripture bears the imprint of Paul on parchment, sent to Timothy, twenty centuries ago. But it is also the Word of God, written for all of us.

This passage holds important truth. The Scripture is inspired by God. It is useful—all of it, not just part of it. It is useful because it corrects us when we are wrong. Sometimes, when I read the Bible, my conscience is pricked, sometimes my self-confidence is shaken, sometimes my pride is assaulted, sometimes I am driven to my knees in prayer. This is because the Bible corrects me, it reproves me, it challenges me.

At other times, when reading the Bible, I am overwhelmed by a sense of comfort and encouragement. The Scripture can affirm what I have done (or refused to do); it can reassure, bless and call the best out of me. The Word is a kind of tutor—a teacher, an instrument of Heaven to transform us into the people He created us to be. It is useful to prepare us, equip us, instruct us and develop us for every good work.

Read the Bible through this lens: It is a supernatural instrument in the hand of God, given to us for our well-being. It is clear that some parts of the Bible are to be literally understood. For example, the Ten Commandments in the book of Exodus are, at face value, literal commands. Look at these three, originally received by Moses and preserved over time for our hearing as well:

Exodus 20:13-15
"Do not murder. Do not commit adultery. Do not steal."

The commands are direct, simple, clear. Readers may quarrel about their merit, but the text is straightforward and doable.

Do not murder. You must not murder. You must not take another life without cause. Life is precious. Human life is created in the image of God, and it is not our place in any arbitrary, capricious or selfish way to terminate someone else's life. No. It is not our place to take someone else's life. You must not murder. There's no quarrel about this prohibition, literally understood. No one, so far as I know, argues for the right to end someone else's life without cause.

Do not commit adultery. Adultery is, sadly, not uncommon. But no one argues that adultery (violating a marriage vow, especially when pursuing sexual relationships) is biblically permissible. This command is neither figurative nor limited to certain contexts in culture or time. Adultery is forbidden. Period.

Do not steal. The Bible gives no permission to take or keep what belongs to others without the owner's consent. Again, we may attempt to rationalize why we have the right to possess what we have not been given permission to receive, but the command literally frames a boundary for human relationships. What is earned or gifted may be kept; what is not must be returned or denied. Period.

I believe most biblical instruction falls into this category of interpretation. The Bible speaks literally to the challenges we face and shows us how to navigate them in a righteous way. In my view, much of the historic narrative of Scripture can reasonably be understood literally, as well. I believe, as an example, that Jonah was actually swallowed by a great fish.

Perhaps you are familiar with the famous Scopes trial in Tennessee in 1925.[2] A local school teacher, John Scopes, was charged with violating state law by introducing evolution into his public school classroom as a way of comprehending the origin and development of human life; Tennessee state law, at the time, forbade such teaching (quite literally). Clarence Darrow, an iconic defense attorney affiliated with the American Civil Liberties Union, joined the Scopes defense team. William Jennings Bryan, three times the Democratic Party's nominee for president, Woodrow Wilson's Secretary of State, and arguably the most effective orator of his time, joined the prosecution team. The trial itself unfolded in circus-like atmosphere, as the nation's attention was riveted not so much on the culpability of Scopes (he was found guilty of violating the law), but on the larger debate between traditionally held views and the emerging (indeed, evolving) science of the preceding 100 years.

In a move that the *New York Times* then described as "the most amazing court scene in Anglo-Saxon history," Darrow (the defense attorney) put Bryan (the prosecutor) on the witness stand, attempting to expose what he believed to be the small-minded and absurdly literal view of biblical history Bryan represented.

The examination of William Jennings Bryan on the stand is a remarkable read. It has been parodied in fiction and cast as the Waterloo of Bryan's long public life; he died, unexpectedly, one week later.

Whatever the conclusion of history might be, Bryan scored some points. Darrow smartly asked Bryan a series of questions designed to ridicule a literal view of Scripture. Bryan was asked if he believed in the integrity of the Bible's historic narratives. Did he believe that the story of Noah and the flood actually took place? Did the sun actually stand still during the lifetime of Joshua? Was Adam literally tempted in a garden called Eden? And so on.

Bryan affirmed that he believed these Bible histories to be quite literally true, representing real people in real time in real events.

The Bible story with which Darrow seemed most preoccupied was the one we have dubbed "Jonah and the Whale" (although the Scripture does not use the term "whale," but "great fish"; see Jonah 1:17). Did Bryan actually believe that Jonah was swallowed by a great fish and then spit out again?

Bryan replied essentially (and I paraphrase here), "Yes, I do quite literally believe that Jonah was swallowed by a whale, and if the Scripture then said the whale was swallowed by Jonah, I'd believe that, too, because one miracle is as easy to believe as another."

Bingo. Bryan's point was well taken. Once you accept the premise of the supernatural—once you consider the miraculous intervention of God in one story legitimate—then why challenge the accuracy of another narrative in the same anthology? What criteria are used to differentiate between the supernatural phenomena recorded in the Bible? If Jesus is a miracle-worker, if Moses can strike a rock and find water, if Hezekiah can see the shadow on his sundial move backward, why quibble about Jonah and the whale?

Perhaps I am a theological Neanderthal, but I believe the histories of the Old and New Testaments are more than illustrative texts, highlighting divine wisdom; I believe they also record and preserve history. If I believe that Jesus literally was nailed to a cross, buried and then rose from the dead (and I do), then I can reasonably believe that the other stories in the Bible describe real events as well.

I realize there are many bright minds who have concluded otherwise. But, even if you do not believe that Jonah was swallowed by a whale, you can still understand that the command prohibiting adultery has literal application in everyday life. Anyone who respects the Bible knows there are commands best read literally, not figuratively.

Does the Bible express truth in ways other than literal histories or specific commands? The Bible communicates truth from heaven to earth; God speaks to us through His Word; He discloses eternal, timeless, infinite truth in ways we can understand and often in the same ways that we communicate with one another.

For instance, if I were to tell you that last week in Anderson, Indiana, where I live, it was "raining cats and dogs," would I be telling you the truth? Would you say, "That cannot be true," or otherwise question the accuracy of my report?

Did anyone actually see domestic pets falling from the sky? No. Did anyone see it raining "cats and dogs?" Yes. The phrase reflects a rainfall of great intensity, a downpour. This kind of rain is not a gentle, caressing, refreshing rain like the Seattle drizzle in which I grew up. No, it is a drenching, torrential rain that gathers in the streets and floods the gutters. In fact, the origin of the expression is thought to be the flooded streets of 17th-century

England, into which heavy rainfalls would literally wash dead cats and dogs. It's a turn of the phrase that now figuratively describes a cloudburst of Noah's Ark-like potential; it is not literally true but still states a truth. Yes, it rained "cats and dogs" in Anderson.

Jesus said, "You are the salt . . ." (Matthew 5:13). Of course, He was describing our capacity to influence, to change the taste of the world in which we live; He was not suggesting that we were literally salt. Like raining "cats and dogs," Jesus' phrase employs vivid—if not literal—imagery to communicate truth.

Language can be very nuanced. We must consider many different cultural and contextual backgrounds to words and phrases in ancient text that can be fairly considered when reading the Bible. We must be careful not to pejoratively label others as unorthodox or less-than-faithful-to-the-truth simply because they understand the meaning of the Word at some points differently than do we. Indeed, the Bible is a collection of Heaven's truth, spoken to earth, using different mediums of language.

There is the literal medium: You shall not commit adultery.

But there is also a figurative medium. Figurative language can be divided into several different categories. For instance, there are *metaphors* in the Scripture. A metaphor is a direct comparison. It speaks a truth, but does so by way of a comparison or representationally.

John 15:1
"I am the true grapevine, and my Father is the gardener."

Jesus here represents Himself as a vine. In the larger context of this passage, He describes how we are the branches and we need to be fixed to the vine. He continues by stating that just as a branch can be cut from a grapevine, wither and die (because divorced from the vine it has no way to sustain its life), so can we be separated from Jesus and perish. This truth is conveyed using a metaphor.

Another way of speaking figuratively is to use a *simile*. A simile is a concept, an illustration, that's introduced with words such as "like," or "as."

Revelation 1:14-15
"His head and his hair were white as wool, as white as snow. And his eyes were like flames of fire. His feet were like polished bronze

refined in a furnace, and his voice thundered like mighty ocean waves."

The Apostle John penned these lines after experiencing a dramatic vision while imprisoned on the island of Patmos in the Mediterranean. The vision was so compelling that he wrote it down for others to read in the New Testament book called Revelation; indeed, he was commanded to do so by a voice from heaven.

John has seen Jesus in this vision. He has seen Jesus before, of course, in Galilee, in Jerusalem, on the Cross, and in His resurrection glory. Now, many years later, he sees Jesus once more, this time indisputably as the King of Kings and Lord of Lords. The Jesus he sees now, however, defies human experience and ordinary description.

And so, John uses a simile to tell us the truth about Jesus. Does anyone really believe that Jesus had eyes of fire, hot and dangerous, with the capacity to scald or burn—a fire like we might use to roast a hot dog on the beach or warm our houses in a fireplace? Of course not. No, John is describing in experiential language something—Someone—far beyond our ability to otherwise comprehend. It cannot be taken literally; it is, nevertheless, true.

Jesus spoke this way often.

Matthew 13:45
"The Kingdom of Heaven is like a merchant on the lookout for choice pearls. When he discovered a pearl of great value, he sold everything he owned and bought it!"

Throughout Matthew 13, we find similes introducing us to the Kingdom of God. Characteristics of the Kingdom appear in clear view as the truth is declared figuratively, unequivocally. The Kingdom of Heaven is not actually a pearl. But it is a priceless treasure that must be sought and found, like a pearl.

The Bible also uses *hyperbole*, exaggeration. Some people believe that exaggerating is equivalent to telling a lie. But hyperbole can be a powerful tool to emphasize and underscore a truth. For example, the Apostle John closes his account of the story of Jesus this way:

John 21:25
"Jesus also did many other things. If they were all written down, I suppose the whole world could not contain the books that would be written."

John emphasizes the volume and vast number of Jesus' astounding works in this world by using hyperbole. Is it literally true that the whole earth could not contain all of the books that might be written tracing Jesus' footsteps? With modern advances in information technology and data management, could we not capture and catalog all of the wonderful things He did in those days when He walked in the flesh with us? Yes, yes, we could. John isn't arguing literally that there isn't space in the world; he's simply saying that he's written a book, and in that book he's selectively chosen highlights of Jesus' most remarkable life. He says in an earlier text that the reason he wrote the book was so that we could know that Jesus is the Christ, and that by believing He is the Christ we can have life in Jesus' name.

That is why John chose the stories recorded in his biography of Christ; he chose these stories to demonstrate that truth to us. But he wanted us to know that there were many more stories he might also have included. He did not have time to write them all down: their number is legion, beyond the capacity of human libraries to fully catalog.

It's hyperbole. It's an exaggeration of a truth to drive home its veracity.

Another use of the language we see in Scripture is what's called *anthropomorphism*. It is a big word that simply means that the divine is reduced to or interpreted through human terms.

2 Chronicles 16:9
"The eyes of the Lord search the whole earth in order to strengthen those whose hearts are fully committed to him. What a fool you have been! From now on you will be at war."

This Scripture is a reproof. But notice how God is described. He's described as having eyes. It's anthropomorphic. He's described in physical and human terms, even though He is a Spirit and beyond our ability to fully comprehend. And yet, God is pictured as having eyes that look over this part of the earth and then that one. Can you now picture a face? Can you imagine the Lord's eyes moving across different continents and countries, peering over the edge of Heaven to see what in fact is going on?

But God is not like that. God is omniscient. He sees everything at once. He sees all the nations at once. He sees all of history at once. He sees this section and that section all at once. He is all knowing. He never sleeps. He never slumbers. He has complete comprehension of all that has been, all that will be, and all that is now. He sees everything, simultaneously, instantaneously.

Anthropomorphism is an attempt to help us, in a tangible way, understand a God who otherwise could not be understood.

The Scripture excels in all of these elements and figures of speech, making the truth shine. How do we differentiate the literal from the figurative and so on?

Well, as a rule of thumb, I suggest that Scripture should be taken literally unless it is obviously and clearly framed otherwise.

- The Kingdom of Heaven is like . . .
- Jesus said, "I am a vine . . ."
- God is described in human terms.
- A parable is introduced as such or clothed with "is like," which introduces a comparison. Jesus is compared to a plant for the purpose of dramatizing an important relational truth. God's omniscience is pictured as equivalent to our amazing, but still finite, human eyes.

The questioner has asked how to differentiate between the various language models employed in Scripture, so here are a few ideas you can keep in mind as you approach the Bible.

First, approach Scripture prayerfully. Never underestimate the power of prayer to guide your thinking. The Bible is a supernaturally authored instrument. God is the Author. When you pray, speak to the Author, engaging the Person who actually wrote the book. Ask Him to help you understand what He has written. He understands your finiteness. He knows that you cannot possibly grasp it all. He knows what your experience has done to dull or compromise your senses. He wants you to have all of the truth you need to live with joy and confidence in this world and in the world to come as well.

Prayer is a mysterious and powerful tool in the pursuit of wisdom. Pray before you read. This must not be a trite ritual; do not open your

Bible without first saying a prayer. In James 1:5, God tells us that if we seek wisdom, He will deliver. But you must believe that He is going to deliver on that promise when you approach Him in prayer. Do not pray, "Lord, help me understand" and then wonder if He'll really help you to understand. Pray as if you believe it and expect Him to answer. You will be surprised how words then seem to jump off the page as you dive into the Word.

Second, seek the life application of the text. Too often, we search the Scriptures but then become distracted by dimensions of the story or its particulars that detour us from the core truth. What were they wearing? Why are these names so difficult to pronounce or remember? What color were the palace walls? Did he trim his beard? How did they build that wall, anyway? The questions can be endless.

These kinds of questions have value, of course. But they can also divert us from the primary reason the Word has been given to us: so that we might know God. We can miss our cues; we can miss the point. What truth in the passage can be applied practically, transformationally or redemptively in our lives? The Bible was written to help us define the world in which we live, our relationship with the God who made us and how we can walk in this world into which He has placed us.

The Bible is a book about life. It is not written to help you understand science, or for us to create other disciplines of knowledge, or even to be an historic tome—though it can provide insight in all of those areas. We read the Bible to find life and how to live it.

As you pray before reading, ask God to help you find the truth you need for everyday life; ask Him also to know how to apply that truth as you go through your day.

It can be very helpful to read the Scripture in a life-application edition or a study Bible. Bibles of this kind place footnotes beneath the sacred text that can guide your thoughts and help clarify meaning. The footnotes may ask questions to help focus your study and apply what you have learned. A Bible commentary can be very useful but is generally limited to understanding historic context, cultural legacy, linguistic research, and other background information. A life-application Bible is designed specifically to assist you as you search for ways to translate the text into your experience.

Life-application study Bibles are available in several different versions. Some of the most popular include the New International Version (NIV), New American Standard Bible (NASB), New King James Version (NKJV) and the New Living Translation (NLT). The notes, helps, questions and life-application articles in each are very useful. Find one that reads easily for you (with the vocabulary, sentence structure and rhythm that best suits your reading style) and dive in.

But do pay attention: some study Bibles have theologically narrow frames that drive their readers to predetermined points of view. Choose a study Bible in the life-application genre and the helps will tend to be more neutral and less doctrinaire.

The New Living Translation Life Application Study Bible (Tyndale, 2004) is the one I recommend most often.

Third, make a commitment to study the context of Scripture, as you decide what passages should be interpreted literally or in some other way. When you begin to understand the world into which the Scripture first came, you will have a much better chance of accurately understanding the Word itself. If you understand what Corinth was like when Paul was writing to the Church of God in Corinth, you will understand many of the Corinthians passages of the New Testament more deeply. You will be better able to appreciate the root principles against the backdrop of ancient culture. You may have to devote yourself to learning some ancient history that heretofore has never interested you. But the Bible has a way of making everything come alive—even history that might have once bored you.

Seeing the Bible on the stage of time, comprehending the world of its origins and identifying timeless truth is a journey—it will not happen suddenly or in the blink of an eye. But over time, you will see the truth of God's Word ever more clearly and be able to differentiate its various literal, figurative, and contextual narratives accurately. It can be done, and you can do it.

To this end, I recommend T*he New Bible Commentary Revised: 21st Century edition* (InterVarsity Press, 2002, G. J. Wenham, J. A. Motyer, D. A. Carson, and R. T. France). In my view, it is the best one-volume commentary available today. I have other commentaries encompassed in as many as 32 volumes, but this is one volume. It is written in the reformed theological tradition, which lands at some different and important points than my own, but it is orthodox, sound and very well done. Remember, it will give you context. When you read about passages that speak about women's hair, for example, the commentary will help you understand the nature of the subject at the time it was written. You can also read how the passage has been interpreted and applied over time. This kind of supplemental reading will greatly enhance your biblical comprehension.

Fourth, decide that you will study the Bible with the Body of Christ. We all need private and personal discipline in the study of God's Word. Never imagine, however, that you can master the Word of God alone. The Body of Christ is the temple of the Holy Spirit, and it is the Holy Spirit who will guide us into all truth (see John 16:13). We need to engage other members of the Body. Your best chance to understand the Scriptures effectively is in the company of other believers.

It is not enough to simply attend a service of Christian worship, week-by-week or from time-to-time. You must involve yourself more intimately in the life of the Body and take some chances in small-group pursuit of God's Word: a Sunday school class, a home study group, a Bible study in the middle of the week, at breakfast, lunch or in the evening. Find a church that gives you some options and then take advantage of them.

Test your ideas and understanding in that small group study. Listen. Ask questions, Wrestle with the answers, together. Wonder, together, whether or not the passage in play should be interpreted literally or figuratively. You will be astonished at the clarity and confidence you can develop with God's Word when you take the risk and become part of the Body of Christ in a small group.

Yes, it can be risky. You may not feel comfortable speaking aloud in a circle of folks you do not know well. You may find it challenging to break into a Bible study, and you may fear you will not fit in. Whatever the obstacles, overcome them. If there is one thing the devil does not want to happen it is for you to connect to a small group studying the Bible.

You may be surprised to find that God gave you a piece of the interpretive puzzle, even as He gave some others in the Body pieces of the puzzle. No one alone will be able to pull the puzzle together until each of us places our piece on the table. And then, as we see how the pieces fit together, we will also see how God's truth should be best understood and applied.

Fifth, work to understand your own context. It is not enough to know about how the Bible was formed, what the world was like when a particular book was written or the experience of the audience to whom the book was originally written.

No, that's not enough. It can be helpful, but it's not enough. You must understand your own context and journey, too. We all bring to the table preconceived notions, subtle prejudices, biases, and 1,001 different kinds of ideas that are subliminally planted in our heads. We all need to know where we have come from, the culture in which we were raised, and we need to come to terms with the journey of our own lives thus far.

Many people have very limited pictures of the Scripture because they've never seen a culture different from their own. They've never expanded beyond what they've always known.

Traveling on a mission trip with other members of the Body of Christ can be one of the greatest Bible study and interpretive tools ever experienced. In another culture, you will have not only the opportunity to learn and bless, you will also see yourself with new eyes and perspective. Your eyes can also be opened to ideas, concepts and power in the Scriptures that you never imagined.

You may have been raised to believe that Christians are prohibited from participating in certain kinds of conduct, only to find that in other cultures, believers are not constrained in the same way. This can lead you to search the Scriptures. You may discover that your upbringing included a hefty dose of traditional boundaries not well grounded in the Bible. We all have a context that defines us; that context may not always be as heavenly focused as we once imagined. Understanding your context can open your eyes to truth in God's Word.

Sixth, be humble. Humility is always a mark of spiritual maturity; it is a prerequisite for any pursuit of truth. The longer we pursue the Word, the more we study the Bible, the more pretentious we can become. The more convinced we are of the breadth of our own Bible knowledge, the more tempted we are to pass by the wisdom of others (who also respect the word with the same zeal and the same sincerity we do).

It is always good to be humble when approaching the Word, acknowledging our limitations and finite understanding. My mind is small. I have a finite capacity to understand the truth of God. I need others to help me sort the truth out. I must never forget that it is unlikely that any of us will figure all of the truth of God out in this life.

If the disciples of Jesus, who walked with Him and listened to Him teach for three years—person to person, face to face—who sat with Jesus at the Last Supper and listened to the greatest teaching ever delivered—could not understand that the Christ would be crucified and then rise again, if those on the road to Emmaus could not understand it even then after all of the excellent instruction they received as the unrecognized Jesus explained the wisdom of the ages to them, then why do we think we will garner wisdom and comprehend God's Word in ways they could not?

We all need to be humble and recognize that we're moving toward truth. We need to respect those moving with us, even if they don't own the same truth in every particular that we do or don't appreciate it the same way that we do. God will honor that and give us more truth the more humble we are. Remember, arrogant pride of any kind becomes a barrier between us and God.

Seventh, accept the Word by faith and act on it by faith. Make a decision that the Bible is God's Word. I approach the Word believing it is supernaturally inspired. I believe it will be proved true in my life, as I act on it by faith.

I pursue these steps:

- Prayerful consideration
- In the context of the body of Christ
- Learning everything I can about the context of Scripture, and my own context
- Humility as I wrestle with it
- Seek the real truth that God has designed for me to have while reading His Word

If I do all of that, then I will come to a point of clarity and action. I will know the truth; I will be able to determine which passages are to be literally understood in my life, and which are not. In either case, I will know the truth God has for me.

I will come to points where I will have to act, taking steps of faith, faith emboldened by the processes and commitments outlined above. And I will take a chance. For Heaven's sake.

For each of us, there will be life applications of the Word.

The questioner asked, "What happens if I find that something I once believed wasn't exactly right? What if I interpreted a passage incorrectly for many years and now I see that it doesn't really mean that? What should I do?"

You have to live up to the truth of what you understand now. If you have a better, more complete understanding of the truth today, you must live up to it today, even if it conflicts with what you once sincerely believed. Do not be afraid to acknowledge that your earlier understanding of the truth may have been flawed, inadequate or misguided. That acknowledgment is also truth. And the truth sets us free.

The truth does not change; God's Word does not change. Our understanding of it can change, though.

The church that I am privileged to serve as pastor is more than 100 years old. Our church family has met in nine different buildings at seven different addresses in the last century. We've been on the north side of town, the east side of town, and now we're on the south side of town. Those different buildings and addresses, taken together, represent many changes over the years.

But our church is not defined by a place, an address or a building. Many things have changed in our history, but one thing has not changed: we have always been a people devoted to the supremacy and the primacy of the Word. I hold deep convictions, grounded in my understanding of the Word. I am still learning, and God is still polishing my grasp of His truth, but the Bible remains at the center of His revelation to me. Studying the Scripture and growing with it is the stuff of a lifetime.

As you commit to the pursuit of truth in Scripture, God will be faithful to provide a light for your path. He will help you sort out the truth and place each passage in its proper place (whether it is truth disclosed in a literal history or command or in figurative or contextualized narrative). Seek and you will find. That is the promise of Jesus. If that promise works anywhere, it works here: Seek the truth in God's Word and you will find it. One day at a time.

Question 1

Homosexuality

*"What does the Bible say about homosexuality?
Should homosexuals attend church and are they Christians?"*

I am not surprised that this question ranked in the top ten or that it rose to become the number one question; it is the conversation of our time. It sweeps across political divides. It sweeps across cultural divides. It sweeps across religious and spiritual divides. Homosexuality is no stranger in the popular media. It is discussed at the office water cooler. Like *All in the Family* in an earlier age, *Modern Family* is more than a sitcom.

And what does the Bible say? Does it speak to this very important question?

Before we explore the Scripture, consider these replies to an on-the-street videographer, posing the question, at random to passersby, "Do you believe homosexuality is sin?"

"Personally I think so, yeah."

"Everyone should have the right to do whatever they want to do as long as it doesn't hurt anyone else."

"Certainly it is, so is murder and adultery. All sin is sin to God."

"I don't think it's fair to target someone for having homosexual relations if we aren't going to put the same target on people who are having premarital or extramarital sex."

"If you believe in God and that God made everything, then God made me, and I'm gay."

In just these few replies, you can see the outlines of the argument. You can see how much of the argument is individually framed by what we feel or think; no one appeals to an objective reference beyond themselves. The question posed was straightforward and the answers given were, for the most part, unequivocal. People tend to have absolute judgment in this area. There are very few responses in the, "I'm not sure," or "My head and heart are torn on this one," vein.

The question asked in this series is tied to the Bible. What does it have to say? It is interesting to note that words like *homosexual* and are themselves relatively new additions to the English language, added in the last 125 years. Previously, the words did not exist; they have evolved over time. However, the premise of homosexuality (a term applied to both men and women), the concept of same gender sexual attraction and relationship, is as old as humanity itself. What does the Bible say?

Let's start at the beginning. The Bible is not a collection of random and unrelated wisdom; it is a book woven with threads of truth from beginning to end. All of us should be wary of building whole systems of thought drawn from single passages. This is especially true when addressing something as fundamental to human identity and experience as our sexuality. We need to search for a continuum of biblical thought, sandwiched between Genesis and Revelation. With this in mind, we will find that the Scripture speaks uniformly, clearly and consistently with one voice on this subject.

Genesis (which means *the beginning*) tells the story of God's creation of the material world. The zenith of His creation was humankind, and Genesis gives us a glimpse of how the development of human life was stepped and sequenced.

> **Genesis 2:18**
> *"Then the Lord God said, 'It is not good for the man to be alone. I will make a helper who is just right for him.'"*

At this moment in the creation narrative, we can see that God has created Adam male, and that He has understood that this man was created in such a way as to need companionship; it is not good for him to be alone. We are created for social interaction. We are wired to crave sharing and intimacy. We are created for relationship. God acknowledges this as He sees the man He has made. We are incomplete alone; we are whole only in relationship. We can ultimately find this wholeness in relationship with God; God created a world in which He models that relationship by placing us in relationship with other created and living beings.

> **Genesis 2:19-20**
> *"So the Lord God formed from the ground all the wild animals and all the birds of the sky. He brought them to the man to see what he would call them, and the man chose a name for each one. He gave names to all the livestock, all the birds of the sky, and all the wild animals. But still there was no helper just right for him."*

It is God's intention, having acknowledged that man should not be alone, to create a helper that is just right for him; not an incidental helper, not a partial helper, but a fully complementary one, a helper that can bring completion, wholeness. The animal kingdom is introduced with its astonishing diversity and beauty, but it is not adequate to make Adam complete, whole. For all of their wonder, animals can go only so far in relating to us. Domesticated animals still play important roles relating to the human family, but no animal can fully compensate for relationship with another human being.

We have an animal that lives in our house, Genesis-the-Wonder-Dog. She's a Jack Russell Terrier that our son Andrew purchased when he was in the eighth grade. Of course, he's in his mid-20s and on his own now; Genesis still lives with my wife and me. Different members of my family have different kinds of relationships with Genesis. Some are whole and satisfying relationships, of a kind. Speaking for myself, I'd prefer not to have a relationship with Genesis at all. I know: harsh. If I wanted to have a dog, Genesis would be the one to have; I'm just not much interested in investing the time and energy required to care for Genesis (adorable and playful and energetic and hungry for my attention as she is . . . but I digress). However, my wife loves Genesis. I know and respect many folks who love their pets deeply, interact with them in profoundly connecting ways, sleep with them, take them out to dinner and all the rest. No problem. But in the end, all of us know that a pet can never be a complete substitute for a person, also created in the image of God. Only people bear the image of God; only people can approach wholeness together.

Genesis 2:21-22

"So the Lord God caused the man to fall into a deep sleep. While the man slept, the Lord God took out one of the man's ribs and closed up the opening. Then the Lord God made a woman from the rib, and he brought her to the man."

Notice the progression: God creates man, acknowledges that man is alone and needs a partner, and then intentionally creates the perfect complement: woman. Two genders are now in play, each created in the image of God. Neither alone can capture all of the dimensions of the divine image, but together they merge the masculine and feminine characteristics of one God. Each gender brings to the table a component of God's image that the other does not possess; together the two can become one, most closely expressing the wonder of the Divine. It should be no surprise, then, that the New Testament repeatedly pictures our relationship with God as a kind of marriage; Jesus is the Bridegroom, the church His bride.

This template defines human relationships.

You can have a close relationship—indeed a fulfilling relationship at many levels—with another person of the same gender, of course. I have some male friends with whom I share a deep level of intimacy. Male friends can understand some things about my life as a man that my wife will never comprehend. I will never be able to know some things she will know as a woman. She is fascinated by childbirth, for instance, and enjoyed being pregnant, bringing to life our four sons. Not my cup of tea. And childbirth? Mostly gross, by my estimation. She, on the other hand, works as a labor and delivery coach, just for fun!

Men tend to be wired differently. I am not drawn to many of the traditionally defined masculine pursuits (like sports, mechanics, hunting, fishing or working with my hands), but I am intensely competitive, always up for a contest, prone to take the dare and seek adventure in classically male ways. I treasure my friendships with other men and can be energized by them. But those same-gender relationships can never bring me the fulfillment, the wholeness and the completeness that a relationship with a woman can bring. That's certainly what the creation record suggests, anyway.

This biblical frame from the dawn of history is affirmed throughout the whole of Scripture. For instance, Jesus Himself interpreted the Bible in this way.

If you're seeking a way to interpret the Bible, if you're looking for a commentary on Scripture, your best bet is the Scripture itself. Refer to and understand one passage by seeing how it is corroborated, understood or polished by another. We have looked at Genesis and how it records the origin of things. Next, we can explore how Jesus interpreted those passages. What did He draw from them?

In Matthew 19, Jesus speaks about these issues. As God, He is the Author of the Word. He was at the beginning; nothing was made without Him. And, in the Gospels, He speaks to us in real time about those events:

> **Matthew 19:4**
> *"'Haven't you read the Scriptures?' Jesus replied. 'They record that from the beginning "God made them male and female." And He said, "this explains why a man leaves his father and mother and is joined to his wife, and the two are united into one." Since they are no longer two but one, let no one split apart what God has joined together.'"*

It's interesting that Jesus emphasizes the two genders and reasons that the intimacy, the union, of two individuals in marriage is the rationale for stepping away from our parents. The reason we leave home is to be joined to someone of the opposite sex. This is proclaimed divinely normative. It is the way God made them, "male and female," "for this purpose."

Marriage is, throughout the New Testament, the superlative metaphor for our union with God. In speaking about marriage, Jesus always and exclusively speaks of it within a heterosexual context, never a homosexual one. Homosexuality was not unknown in the days Jesus walked this earth; still He never embraces it in His references to marriage or sexuality—subjects to which He was no stranger. The Bible, as a whole, never does, either. Jesus is the ultimate commentary on God's Word; He is the Word. "For this reason," He reminds us, "a man leaves . . . for his wife."

I believe, in the first instance, Jesus speaks here of the physical reality that the male physique is designed to fit together with the female physique, joining two as one. At a deeper level, I think He also speaks of the way in which a man and a woman, having joined together physically, can experience a kind of union of soul and spirit that cannot be replicated in any other relationship in this material world. A sexual union can be superficially consummated on simply a physical plane. It can also be experienced with extraordinary depth on several levels, as it conforms to God's original design within marriage. In biblical terms, a sexual partnership requires both a man and a woman.

Some have argued, "But, Jesus never spoke about homosexuality. If He did not endorse it, He certainly did not condemn it." This is true. But He did speak often about sexuality and about marriage, always affirming it, always esteeming it. He did not speak about incest, either, or threesomes, or any number of other sexual combinations that could be named, but this is not an argument to say He approves of them. What He did say was consistent with the rest of Scripture: A sexual relationship requires that you leave your parents and marry your wife (or, by extension, your husband). He affirmed heterosexual marriage; that's the only kind of sexual relationship He affirmed; He spoke with clarity and without equivocation or exceptions to the rule.

This principle is expanded in other parts of the New Testament. There are Old Testament passages that line up with this view, as well.

> **Leviticus 18:20-23**
> *"Do not defile yourself by having sexual intercourse with your neighbor's wife. Do not permit any of your children to be offered as a sacrifice to Molech, for you must not bring shame on the name of your God. I am the Lord. Do not practice homosexuality, having sex with another man as with a woman. It is a detestable sin. A man must not defile himself by having sex with an animal. And a woman must not offer herself to a male animal to have intercourse with it. This is a perverse act."*

This passage is drawn from what's called the Holiness Code. It is a section found in a larger list of rules and regulations that God specifically gives to the Hebrews, so that they might be differentiated from the people who claimed the land of Canaan as home. Verse 22 speaks of homosexuality specifically and defines it. All of these rules are markers, setting God's people apart from the world around them. Sexual conduct is one of the most important markers.

First, adultery is forbidden. God's people are prohibited from sexual relationships with others to whom they are not married. Sexual relationship outside of marriage was endemic, customary and viewed as normative in the pagan world of Israel's neighbors. But God insisted that His people be different. He as much as said, "No, you are a holy people, My people. You will honor your spouse by being sexually exclusive."

Second, sacrifices to the god Molech were prohibited. Molech was one of the region's ancient gods, an idol handmade. The worship of Molech often involved the murder and sacrifice of children. The extraordinary devotion displayed by the murder of one's own children was esteemed and praised. Again, God insists that His people be different. "No, you will not do what those who worship Molech do; you will not murder children in worship; you will not shed their blood; to do so brings shame on My Name."

Third, homosexuality is condemned. Same gender sexual engagements were prevalent and accepted as an ordinary part of social life in the ancient neighborhood of the Hebrews. Once more, God draws a line across which His people are forbidden to cross. "No. You will not commit adultery; men will not be sexually active with women to whom they are not married and women will not be sexually active with men to whom they are not married. Furthermore, you will not murder your children as a sacrifice to Molech. And you must not practice homosexuality, engaging in sexual relationships with persons of the same gender. It is detestable; it is forbidden." God separates His people from the world around them. His boundaries are clear, explicit and precise.

The Lord continues, in this passage, by forbidding bestiality. God's people must never see animals as sexual objects or partners. Bestiality, like the other forms of sexual conduct proscribed above, was not unknown in the ancient world; it formed part of the religious rituals of some pagan cultures, not surprising, as idols often reflected animal forms. Again, God sets His people apart by requiring a different sexual ethic than is prevalent elsewhere. How human sexuality is to be pursued, experienced and understood was a primary marker in the Old Testament world, defining holiness. This was true in the first century of the Christian era, too.

The ancient Greek and Roman civilizations that framed the New Testament world were as pagan and sexually charged as the ancient Egyptian, Canaanite and Mesopotamian cultures that preceded them and framed the Old Testament world. The Christian community's sexual ethic was, arguably, the most singular and dramatic way in which it was differentiated from the pagan culture that thrived all around it. The Christian community's sexual ethic, grounded in the revelation of God's

Word, was then, as it is becoming once more today, decidedly countercultural, at odds with prevailing norms. It's curious how in modern times, we find ourselves wrestling still with this defining boundary, wondering if the traditionally understood biblical view of human sexuality is really so necessary, after all. As long as we express ourselves lovingly and enjoy sexual relationships that are consensual, are we not congruent with the spirit of Scripture? Does gender really matter? Isn't it unfair to place homosexuality in a list that also includes adultery, bestiality, and ritual murder?

Some contend that the Leviticus passage is not determinative, because it stands not so much against the behaviors condemned but the idolatrous worship they exalt. Some argue that this holiness code was necessary only so far as the Hebrews needed to be separated from the pagans around them; in a modern world in which such pagan worship is no longer practiced, the ancient prohibitions are no longer required. We have other—and better—ways to set ourselves apart, to practice holiness.

If this train of thought is followed, however, are not all of the sexual barriers suspect? If homosexuality is now permitted, is bestiality, also? Consensual sex between unmarried partners? If animals are protected and not injured by a sexual encounter, why not? By what criteria is one prohibition discarded and another still honored? How is one boundary contextualized and another not? No one is arguing for child sacrifice, so far as I know. Bestiality (now also referred to as zoophilia) flies only under the radar in most places, and I am not aware of any serious movement to legalize it in the United States. But, as everyone knows, homosexuality has become mainstreamed. From the vantage point of this text, there is no consistent logic in doing so.

But wait, Leviticus is filled with rules and regulations that Christians do not now observe. Are we not set free from the Old Testament ceremonial laws? Are there not many Old Testament boundaries that were designed for the social order of the ancient Hebrews alone and that do not now have bearing on us? Can't this narrow view of sexual conduct be seen in that category? Have they not passed away? Now that Jesus has come, do we not have freedom? Has not the old passed away and the new come?

No. In the Old Testament, there was ceremonial law, which we no longer observe. For example, observance of circumcision, dietary regulations, and Old Testament holy days and festivals are no longer binding in the New Testament age. The Scripture specifically addresses these. But the moral law—the law that governs relationships between persons and our God—has not changed. Indeed, it is affirmed by the New Testament, as it was proclaimed in the Old.

So what does the New Testament say about homosexuality?

> **1 Corinthians 6:9-11**
> *"Don't you realize that those who do wrong will not inherit the Kingdom of God? Don't fool yourselves. Those who indulge in sexual sin, or who worship idols, or commit adultery, or are male prostitutes, or practice homosexuality, or are thieves, or greedy people, or drunkards, or are abusive, or cheat people - none of these will inherit the Kingdom of God. Some of you were once like that. But you were cleansed; you were made holy; you were made right with God by calling on the name of the Lord Jesus Christ and by the Spirit of our God."*

Here the Apostle Paul is writing to the young Christian community in ancient Corinth. One of the wealthiest, most naturally beautiful, strategically located, and favored cities of the Roman Empire, Corinth was famed, even by ancient standards, for its sexual license. Across the Roman Empire it was widely known by those traveling for business or pleasure that Corinth was the place to stop for a good time. Devoted to the worship of the Greek goddess of love and sexuality, Aphrodite (the Romans named her Venus), the Corinthians lived easily with a cult of sacred prostitution, in which random sexual encounters were seen as worship of the goddess. Evenings were invitations to worship in this way, with as many as 1,000 temple prostitutes available daily. Straight and gay sex were viewed as normative; most men would have bisexual histories, often within the context of rite-of-passage pairings between young men advancing through puberty and "older men" (usually in their 20s). These pairings were not exclusively sexual or religious in nature, but routinely included a sexual component. It was into this sexually charged environment that the Church of God in Corinth was born; it was in this milieu that the church's counter-cultural sexual ethic would distinguish it.

Paul speaks to a Christian community quite familiar with the popular view of sexuality, with few prohibitions. He speaks to a population that has been raised to believe, before being introduced to the Gospel, that such sexual license was normal and healthy. In fact, he reminds them, "You once used to be like that, but now you have been redeemed. You have been changed." It is possible to be changed, to be called from one way of life to another. The Corinthian church had done so in the power and presence of Christ—while still living in the shadow of the temple of Aphrodite.

As with the Leviticus passage, step back one frame and review the list of distinctives. This list captures criteria for a holy people. Notice how holiness has often been defined over the years by lists different from this one—lists that suggest boundaries that are nowhere mentioned here (or anywhere else in the Bible). Much time and energy has been wasted wringing our hands over prohibitions that God has not prohibited in His Word and diminishing the boundaries He has set in place. Imagine how the church would be empowered if we made it our ambition to simply live up to the commands of this list.

First, God calls us to be a people who do not indulge in sexual sin. First and foremost, we are to be a people who learn how to manage our sexual selves. This requires us to acknowledge that God has given us the capacity to manage our sexual natures, conduct and expression. We are not powerless in the face of temptation or unacceptable sexual desire. We are not lower beings without ability to govern our sexuality. We are not slaves to sexual impulse unless we chose to be. This truth was especially relevant for the Corinthians then—as it is for us today.

Second, we must not to worship idols. We must worship God alone, acknowledging His supremacy in our world and individual lives. We must not bow before other gods, becoming morally subject to laws contravening His own.

Third, God prohibits adultery. We must be committed to our marriage vows for a lifetime. Sexual fidelity in marriage is at the core of the marriage commitment.

Fourth, we must not prostitute ourselves (men are here named; later in this same chapter, female prostitution is also forbidden). We must not sell our bodies or trade them for favors; we will not use our sexuality for economic gain.

Fifth, God forbids his people from practicing homosexuality. The original Greek word here translated into English as *homosexuality* is the combination of two words that literally mean: male, to lie with sexually, have intercourse. This is prohibited.

Sixth, we must not steal; we must not take what does not belong to us.

Seventh, greed is forbidden. It is clear we should not be materially oriented, always aggregating more and more things for ourselves.

Eighth, God will not tolerate drunkenness; we must not become inebriated, losing self-control.

Ninth, we are told not to be abusers and swindlers, taking advantage of others, cheating or otherwise.

What if we focused on this list and, by the grace of God, lived up to it? What if an entire community of believers made this their ambition and lived within these boundaries? Would they be recognized as a distinct and separate people, in the world but not of the world? Yes, they would be. Yes, we could be.

Sadly, we are too often diverted from this high calling by one hundred and one other things—controversies over conduct that are not on this list.

As with the Old Testament references to homosexuality, there are some voices that challenge a straightforward reading of this New Testament prohibition, as well. The argument sometimes is made that a modern concept of an exclusively monogamous homosexual relationship was not in view at the time the Corinthian letters were written. This reasoning contends that the Scripture refers to temple prostitution and occult practice only—or, perhaps, the ancient Greek custom of man-boy developmental social and sexual relationships. In either case, the Bible cannot be speaking about the whole, healthy and committed same-gender sexual relationships, nourished in a loving, lifetime context that are esteemed today. Others argue that Paul's original Greek, with which he wrote this letter, is obscure and uncertain.

I am not persuaded.

If any passage in the Bible can be said to be clear, this one can—in all cultures, in all languages, in all generations, in all time. Throughout twenty centuries of Christian history, in nearly two millennia of profound theological and academic research across all branches of the Christian family—Roman Catholic, Eastern Orthodox, and Protestant—all have agreed about what it means. It refers to sexual conduct between people of the same gender, translated today in our English language as homosexual. Only very recently (as measured by centuries in the New Testament age) has the plain statement of the text been challenged substantively; it has, for the vast majority of church scholars, never been challenged persuasively.

To argue that the passage is no longer in force or that it does not apply to our contemporary context poses the same difficulties when measuring the New Testament as it does the Old. How do we pick and choose from the list of nine distinguishing marks? If the homosexual boundary is to be set aside, how about the one dealing with adultery? Theft? Abuse? Prostitution? Am I free to take advantage of you in the 21st century, because the 1st-century audience to whom the text was first written lived in a different world requiring different moral parameters?

No, the case is just too weak to be sustained. There is a consistent thread throughout the Scripture on this subject, in both Testaments. Look next at the New Testament book of Romans.

In this stunningly direct passage, Paul speaks with a power and an edge that is, frankly, hard for me to bear. It is hard for me to imagine myself writing in this way, in this tone. But Romans is indisputably as supernaturally inspired as any other book in the canon; Paul's astonishing intellect and deep spirituality are everywhere on display from its beginning to its end. He describes a world in which people have abandoned God in the pursuit of their own will and way, believing that their own understanding trumps the revealed Word. And then he writes:

> **Romans 1:26-27**
> *"That is why God abandoned them to their shameful desires. Even the women turned against the natural way to have sex and instead indulged in sex with each other. And the men, instead of having normal sexual relations with women burned with lust for each other. Men did shameful things with other men, and as a result of this sin, they suffered within themselves the penalty they deserved. Since they thought it foolish to acknowledge God, he abandoned them to their foolish thinking and let them do things that should never be done."*

It is hard to read; it is hard to hear; it is hard to think of friends—sometimes family—who have sorted out their lives differently, in opposition to this text. The passage is so sharp, so unequivocal and absolute, that it is hard to hold it in one hand while holding precious souls who have embraced homosexuality as somehow a God-blessed, God-ordained course, in the other.

It is hard for them to read this, as it speaks so starkly about the right and wrong of it, about the consequence of it, and about the way in which lives hang in the balance. There is little room to maneuver, as the text, in no uncertain terms, describes how God steps away from those who pursue sexual relationships with others of the same gender. It declares that where we land on this subject is one of those defining markers, disclosing whether we are just in the world or actually of the world. I admit that it's a tough one to preach these days, a difficult one to bear.

But then I have been reconciled to this larger truth: In life, all of us must make a decision about truth and its objective reality apart from our own feelings, our hoped-for outcomes, our sense of the way things should be.

How I wish that I could find a Bible passage that could help me argue that homosexuality is acceptable by the light of Heaven. How I wish I could say it doesn't really matter what people do in the privacy of their own home, if done lovingly. How I wish I could say to everyone, "Just do as you please, with whomever you please, as long as you do it consensually and no one gets hurt." How I wish I could think of some of the brightest and brilliant people I know who believe they are homosexuals and not also think they are outside the will of God. Life would be so much simpler then, wouldn't it?

But I cannot, because I have adopted the Bible as my guide. I believe it is the Word of God, unchanging, pure, true. I have learned over time that the best outcomes in life uniformly are found when I defer to that Word. It is an objective standard beyond myself that cannot be changed by me, amended by me or turned on its head by me. Ultimately, I believe the Lord will measure my life by it; until then, I must measure my life by it, as well

The Bible can have a hard edge sometimes; it can cut as well as heal. My observation, however, looking over centuries of human experience, is that it remains the single most credible platform of objective truth. Wherever life takes you, your chance of success and wholeness are enhanced more by the Bible than by any other resource you can hold in your hand or heart.

When holding the Bible, we have two ways to approach it. We can attempt to define the Bible by our experience; we can attempt to conform its precepts to what we have already known experientially. Alternately, we can define our experience by the Bible; we can attempt to conform our experience to what the Bible commends. These are quite different pathways that will net quite different outcomes. I vote for the latter, even though it requires more trust and faith.

And so that is what I reach for. I have made the case here, albeit limited by just a cursory review of the relevant Scriptures, that the Bible does not permit homosexual practice within the Kingdom of God. Indeed, expressing your sexuality within a homosexual paradigm separates you from that Kingdom and from God. Still, having said that, I do not contend that those who believe themselves to be homosexual have chosen to be homosexual.

It is not as simple as that.

Our behavior patterns and the ways in which we think about ourselves is a very complex weave. I think very few people make a conscious decision to be straight or homosexual, in the way people decide to be Republicans or Democrats, doctors or teachers, or even Christians or followers of some other faith. No one wakes up one day and says, "I'll decide to be gay today," or "I think I'll be straight," or "I choose to be lesbian." Life does not work that way—especially life at the core of our being, which is where our sexuality resides.

I do not believe it is possible to understand homosexuality without considering the larger issue of human sexuality per se. Sexual identity is a fundamental part of our persona. Its development is affected by myriad factors (material, physical, experiential, circumstantial, spiritual, mental, emotional, relational) over the course of a lifetime, particularly in our childhood and adolescent years. Some of these developmental influences are consciously understood; others are subliminal, but nonetheless powerful (and, perhaps, more so).

Why do any of us have sexual preferences of any kind? Why do some men prefer women with large breasts as sexual partners, while others favor a comely rear end? Why do some women find tall, dark and muscular attractive, and others desire blond and lean? What are the origins of pedophilia? Are some "born that way?" Why do some relish oral sex and others find it detestable? The questions are legion. We can answer these questions only by coming to some conclusions about the formation of our sexual appetites. It is a complex weave.

All of us struggle with something in life. All of us have some kind of soul wrestling—wrestling matches in which we sometimes feel caught in the middle. We are uncomfortable with a course of action or thought; the moral plumb line by which we measure ourselves (in this case, the Bible) is not congruent with our conduct. And yet, we continue on the same course, confused or condemned or both, feeling compelled to do wrong, in a way, and, at the same time, longing to do right. We may feel trapped in this wrestling match. The spirit is willing, but the flesh is weak.

We can conclude that we are created with this natural predisposition to do what we fear is not allowed. We begin to ask, "What kind of God would create me this way and the require me to act against my created preference? Surely, a loving God would not create me to thirst after this or that and then condemn me for reaching to satisfy my thirst, would He?" As we progress in this way, we are prone to surrender to the flesh before we consider surrendering to the spirit.

All of us are born into a world that has been corrupted by sin; consequently, every one of us will have a broken place or two, or ten, with which we'll wrestle.

I have not struggled with my sexual orientation. I am a straight, heterosexual man—and glad to be one. I have not been troubled with questions wondering if I was really a gay man suppressing my native desire to satisfy a religious or social mandate.

Because I have not struggled with my orientation is not the same as saying I have not struggled. I have had other challenges that have caused me to wonder, "Why was I made this way?" or "Why am I like this?" Then, I have to stop and wonder, "Was I really made this way, or have I just developed this way?" What part of my struggle is my native wiring and what part is my environmental and experiential conditioning? What part of it is really about my will?

I am not going to ask for a show of hands, but how many men, reading this book, would—if you felt free to do so, without anyone thinking less of you or disparaging your character as a consequence of your response—raise your hand with me and say, "I don't get it. Why would I ever even consider looking at pornography? Why would I do that? Why have I been wired to be so visually stimulated by people I don't even know? Why would I spend any time in a fantasy land that can only take my imagination into places that can produce no good in my life or anyone else's? What's up with that? Why am I like this?"

How many men on the planet have not been subject to this temptation? I contend that every man alive is subject to this temptation, admit it or not. You do not have to succumb to the temptation to wonder why it can stalk you. Do you know why? It is because you are wired that way. You are wired to be visually stimulated. Chemicals are released in your brain that give you a kind of high as your sexual thought patterns kick in. How many men have, in exasperation, shaken their fists at Heaven and asked, "Why did you make me a raging hormone? What were you thinking? Couldn't you have created me differently? Couldn't you have made it easier for me? Why did you make me a raging hormone when I was 18 when I wasn't going to get married until I was 26 and then tell me to just manage it?"

But is that the same as saying that because I have this natural predisposition—because I was made male, made to be visually stimulated, made with an aggressive sexual appetite—I should surrender to it because it feels natural to me? Why not just go with it as long as I don't hurt anybody else? What's the problem? Those people who are on the Internet or making those movies are getting paid. They're making good money, a lot more than I'll ever see in a lifetime. What's the problem anyway? It's all consensual. It's just the way I am."

The problem is that I have embraced an objective guidebook for life, inspired, I believe, by God, which tells me I cannot even look with sexual interest at women who are not my wife. I have chosen to live by that biblical standard. It's not always easy, and it does not always come naturally, but it does bring life. I have to wrestle, sometimes to exhaustion and repeatedly, but, as God is my helper, it is a match I can win.

How about you who wrestle with eating too much? Or you who can't drive by the casino without wanting to pull in every night and wager more than you can afford? Or you who struggle with some other behavior? You who gossip? Or lie?

We're all broken aren't we? All of us struggle with something.

But, would any of us say that any of those other troubles should be accepted just because they're a part of us? No.

We are not animals. We are created in the image of God, and we have a capacity to manage our sexuality. It may not be easy, but it can be done.

I know people who have lived for 10 or 15 years as active gay adults in sexual relationships—some monogamous and some not—who have had intersections with God where they were transformed and became straight. That's not to say everyone who wrestles in this area will have this same outcome or that such an outcome can be achieved quickly or easily. But it can be done. Do you know anyone who has given up smoking? It can be a rough road, but it can be done. Even when smoke-free for years, the craving for tobacco can still surprise and dare, from time to time. But smoking can still be conquered.

Isn't it true for all of us that God can change us and renew us? Until we are free from this broken world, we will be exposed to the devil's business, as he seeks to rob, steal and destroy. Ah, but this brings us back to another passage in Romans, like the one we just read earlier.

Romans 7:24-25
"Oh, what a miserable person I am! Who will free me from this life that is dominated by sin and death? Thank God! The answer is in Jesus Christ our Lord. So you see how it is: In my mind I really want to obey God's law, but because of my sinful nature I am a slave to sin."

Romans 8:9
"But you are not controlled by your sinful nature. You are controlled by the Spirit if you have the Spirit of God living in you. (And remember that those who do not have the Spirit of Christ living in them do not belong to him at all.)

Romans 8:12
"Therefore, dear brothers and sisters, you have no obligation to do what your sinful nature urges you to do. For if you live by its dictates, you will die. But if through the power of the Spirit you put to death the deeds of your sinful nature, you will live. For all who are led by the Spirit of God are children of God."

Stop accepting the lie that you can't be different than you are. Stop believing that transformation is the stuff of other people's testimonies and not your own. If you are a believer, the Spirit is in you. And whether your struggle is expressing a homosexual lifestyle or diving into pornography or gambling your life's future away or eating too much and abusing your own body, which is the temple of the Holy Spirit, or you name it . . . God will honor your quest for life-change, for the better, for your own good, for Heaven's sake.

You can be changed.

Should people who struggle with their orientation come to church? Absolutely.

So should everyone who struggles with anything in life—we should all be seeking the Lord's blessing and will together, week-by-week, as the church gathers. Everyone who wrestles with unhealthy diet, the tendency to gossip, the thirst for unhealthy sex—gay or straight—everyone should feel welcome and be welcomed by the church. All of us struggle with something.

It does not matter from where you come or where you have been. What matters is where you want to go. Not where you are, but where you want to go.

Do you want to go with God? Trust Him. Trust His Word.

For every person reading this book thinking, "You don't understand," I admit, I don't understand your case. But then, you don't understand mine either. That aside, you are loved.

I know there are people in my church who are precious to me, who struggle right in front of me in the pew every Sunday. And you know I love you. And the church loves you. And God loves you.

But I can never help someone—I can never love someone—by telling them that what the Bible says is wrong is right. Human sexuality is an extraordinary gift from God; when managed by the light of His Word, it has the power to bless and encourage beyond human understanding. If, however, pursued outside of the Lord's design, it can never satisfy.

We are called to be holy. We are called to be distinctly Christian. From the most ancient time until the present day, our sexual ethic will, as much as anything else, mark us as the Lord's own. Homosexuality separates us from God, not the world. The Bible does not give it license.

Epilogue

Several times each year, I stand before my congregation at Madison Park and take questions. It's pretentiously dubbed the Pastor's Press Conference. There are no members of the press there, of course, but members of our church family show up and ask questions. It is advertised as a question-and-answer hour without limits; any question, on any subject, may be posed.

I do not presume or pretend to have all of the answers. The answers I attempt to provide may prove helpful in the moment; but the primary reasons for the Press Conference are twofold: (1) to practically demonstrate that the Bible has an answer for any question we might dream up, and (2) to underscore that the church is a safe place to ask questions—and should be the first place we visit when questions arise.

The Bible does have an answer for any question you can conceive. It may have a specific reply. For instance, if the question is, "Should I steal the Hershey bar?" the answer is plainly given: "You shall not steal." For many questions, though, it provides a principle from which we might deduce an answer. "Should I marry Susie?" might be answered by a series of Scriptures that can help you determine your eligibility for marriage, the responsibilities of marriage, the process of discerning whether Susie is just right for you—and you for her—and how to find assurance as you make the decision.

Some answers are simple and clear; others are more nuanced. In the end, though, the Bible is a trustworthy, all-around guide for life.

Questions at the Press Conference can be wide ranging. I've been asked everything from, "Is masturbation a sin?" to "Why can't I park my car in front of the Main Auditorium doors?" to "How do I forgive my ex-husband who has left me by the curb and moved in with another woman?" to "Are events in Egypt a sign of the Lord's return?" and more. Participants have the option of writing their questions on paper and submitting them anonymously, minimizing the questioner's potential embarrassment; the questions are randomly drawn from a basket.

I've been embarrassed, fumbling for an on-the-spot answer at times, but the freedom and life that comes from the free-wheeling pursuit of answers—and finding them within a biblical framework—more than compensates for the risks assumed.

This book has focused on just ten questions. My answers may be only starting points for further exploration. Whatever your judgment of the answers given, know that God is willing to take your questions on, anytime. His church should be, too. We may not always agree on the answer or how to best interpret the Scripture, but as long as it is the playing field for our pursuit of truth, we will end well.

Thanks to all those who helped bring this project to life. Sandi Patty would not rest until I tackled a book; her encouragement always has been priceless. Natalie Farmer, Anna Trent, Nicole Carpenter, and Mike Atkins at the Stylos Records and Mike Atkins Entertainment Groups have inspired, believed, and been patient to the last. It could not have been done without you. Kevin Majeski and Ryan Woolsey were instrumental in both the conception and execution of the *Go Ahead. Ask Anything.* surveys and sermon series; Kevin's design work for this book has been superb. To my wife, Maureen: Well, words cannot express my deep appreciation for your support and love in all that I do, this included. And, at the last, to our third son, Andrew Lyon, without whom *Go Ahead. Ask Anything.* would have been lost in a sermon archive rarely visited. His investment and vision cannot be overstated.

Thanks to Word Distribution, also. How proud I am to have been brought into your family; it is distinguished company.

And finally, thanks to you for reading through to the end. Send me your thoughts, if you'd like: AskAnything@PastorJimLyon.com. Go Ahead. Ask Anything.

"If you need wisdom, ask our generous God,
and he will give it to you.

He will not rebuke you for asking.
But when you ask him, be sure that your faith is in God alone.

Do not waver, for a person with divided loyalty
is as unsettled as a wave of the sea
that is blown and tossed by the wind.

Such people should not expect to receive anything from the Lord."

— James 1:5-7

References

Introduction

1. Thanks to John and Tim Worthen for permission to use their names and our Europe trip to make my point.
2. http://www.marshillchurch.org/

Chapter 10: Illegal Immigration

1. http://2010.census.gov/2010census/data/ (accessed April 17, 2011).
2. Jeffrey S. Passel and D'Vera Cohn. *Trends in Unauthorized Immigration: Undocumented Inflow Now Trails Legal Inflow.* Washington, DC: Pew Hispanic Center, October 2008; http://pewhispanic.org/files/reports/94.pdf (accessed April 17, 2011).
3. Jeffrey S. Passel and D'Vera Cohn. "U.S. Unauthorized Immigration Flows Are Down Sharply Since Mid-Decade," Washington, DC: Pew Hispanic Center (September 1, 2010); http://pewhispanic.org_files_report_126.pdf/ (accessed April 17, 2011).
4. http://www.usatoday.com/money/economy/2006-04-10-immigrants-economic-impact_x.htm (accessed April, 17 2011).
5. Jeffrey S. Passel and D'Vera Cohn. "U.S. Unauthorized Immigration Flows Are Down Sharply Since Mid-Decade," Washington, DC: Pew Hispanic Center (September 1, 2010). http://pewhispanic.org_files_report_126.pdf/ (accessed April 19, 2011).
6. http://data.worldbank.org/country/canada (accessed April 17, 2011).
7. According to the US census (http://www.census.gov/hhes/socdemo/language/data/acs/ACS-12.pdf, accessed April 18, 2011), more than 34 million people in America speak Spanish regularly at home. Add to that the more than 9 million undocumented Spanish speaking persons (80% of 12 million, see Figure 2 in the chapter text) and the total is 43 million Spanish speakers in America, which rivals other large Spanish populations of Spanish speaking countries including Spain at 46 million, Columbia at 44 million, and Argentina at 41 million (https://www.cia.gov/library/publications/the-world-factbook/geos/ar.html, accessed April 18, 2011).
8. Statistics from http://pewhispanic.org/files/factsheets/19.pdf (accessed April 18, 2011).
9. http://www.usimmigrationsupport.org/immigrants-send-money-home.html (accessed April 18, 2011).
10. For more information about the India Gospel League and how you can get involved, visit http://www.iglworld.org/

Chapter 9: God: The Decider?

1. The Kerr family has graciously given permission for use of this story in the hope that it might help bring insight and peace to others struggling with confusion and grief.
2. The Owen family has graciously given permission for the use of this story in the hope that it might bring peace and comfort to all those who grieve.
3. Thanks Maureen, for supporting me in all that I do and for allowing your story to be used to bring clarity and strength to all who struggle with brokenness.
4. Matthew 27:46. This Scripture quotation is taken from THE HOLY BIBLE, NEW INTERNATIONAL VERSION®, NIV® Copyright © 1973, 1978, 1984, 2011 by Biblica, Inc.™ Used by permission. All rights reserved worldwide.

Question 8: Sex, Church and Straight Talk

1. http://www.reuters.com/article/2007/05/18/us-hongkong-bible-idUSHKG31748020070518?feedType=RSS (accessed April 19, 2011) The petition was created as backlash to a government censorship on a student survey which asked questions regarding incest and bestiality. Though the petitioner's intent may not have been to actually ban the Bible, the fact remains that the Bible is sexually explicit enough to warrant such a petition.
2. Jerry Ropelato. "2006 & 2005 US Pornography Industry Revenue Statistics." TopTenREVIEWS. 2006. http://internet-filter-review.toptenreviews.com/internet-pornography-statistics.html, accessed April 26, 2011, as quoted in Covenant Eyes Pornography Statistics report (see http://www.covenanteyes.com/).
3. Free Speech Coalition. "White Paper: Report on the Adult Entertainment Industry" 2005, Docstoc http://www.docstoc.com/docs/6117965/Free-Speech-Coalition-WHITE-PAPER-A-Report-on-the, accessed April 26, 2011. See also Washington Times. "MSNBC-Stanford-Duquesne Study," January 26, 2000. Quoted. in "Internet Safety & Children." UT-Dallas Police Department Crime Prevention, October 12, 2008, http://www.utdallas.edu/police/documents/crimeprevention/Internet%20Safety%20&%20Children.pdf, accessed April 26, 2011.
4. Free Speech Coalition, "White Paper: Report on the Adult Entertainment Industry."
5. Michael Leahy, Porn University: What College Students Are Really Saying About Sex on Campus (Chicago: Northfield Publishers, 2009), 55.
6. Jill Manning, Testimony at Hearing on Pornography's Impact on Marriage & the Family; Subcommittee on the Constitution, Civil Rights and Property Rights; Committee on Judiciary; U. S. Senate, November 10, 2005. http://www.heritage.org/research/family/upload/85273_1.pdf, accessed December 8, 2009.

Question 7: Death and What's Next

1. http://www.hammeruncut.com/realtime-death-toll-counter/ (accessed April 20, 2011) The statistics on this site are based on numbers from the World Health Organization found at http://www.who.int/mip/2003/other_documents/en/causesofdeath.pdf (accessed April 20, 2011). Though they are based on data from 2001, the information is still eye opening, and we can assume that annual mortality rates have risen in the past decade along with dramatic increases in the global population.
2. Every reasonable effort has been made to locate the family of Iva Devine for permission to use this story. Please contact the publisher (Stylos Records, 2701 Enterprise Dr., Suite 211; Anderson, IN 46013) with any information on permissions. Updated information will be included in future editions of the book.

Question 6: Choice and Destiny

1. Thanks, Mom, for permission to use your name and our wonderful relationship to help illustration God's love in new and creative ways.
2. http://www.nrf.com/modules.php?name=News&op=viewlive&sp_id=918 (accessed April 20, 2011).
3. http://www.ourdocuments.gov/doc.php?flash=true&doc=61&page=transcript (accessed April 20, 2011). This quotation is taken from Wilson's address to a joint session of Congress, April 2, 1917.

Question 5: The Voice of God

1. Thanks, Kelley, for permission to share your part in this story (bad humor aside), in the hope that others may hear the voice of God in their times of joy and need.

Question 4: The Irreversible Gift

1. Thanks to Mom and to Marguerite's children—my cousins Janet, Fred, and Diane—for letting me use this story to illustrate this important truth.

Question 3: Christianity Compared

1. I do not have a single source for much of the content contained in this chapter. Much of the content in this chapter has been gleaned over my adult lifetime, learning about competing systems in response to questions and challenges in the ministry, and from my travels abroad (spending much time in Hindu India, the Islamic world, and at the birthplace of Buddhism at Sarnath (in India). If you are interested in learning more, I recommend Dean Halverson's *Compact Guide to World Religions* (Bloomington, Minn.: Bethany House, 1996) coupled with any of the resource guides provided by InterVarsity Christian Fellowship: http://www.intervaristy.org/ism/cat/45.
2. *New World Translation of the Holy Scriptures*. Copyright © 2011 Watch Tower Bible and Tract Society of Pennsylvania. All Rights Reserved. (http://www.watchtower.org, accessed April 19, 2011).

Question 2: Applying Scripture

1. More information about the Church of God is available online at http://www.chog.org/.
2. Information about the Scopes trial is taken from John Thomas Scopes, *The World's Most Famous Court Trial,* Lawbook Exchange Edition (Cincinnati: National Book Company, 2010), 284–304.

Listen to Jim Lyon weekly on the radio program *ViewPoint*, a part of the CBH: Christians Broadcasting Hope family of radio programs.

To listen online and find information about *ViewPoint* in your area, visit ww.CBHViewPoint.org

CBH: Christians Broadcasting Hope
PO Box 2420
Anderson, IN 46018-2420

Ask More Questions and Connect with Jim Lyon

Web site: www.PastorJimLyon.com
Twitter: @PastorJimLyon
Facebook: facebook.com/PastorJimLyon
Email: AskAnything@PastorJimLyon.com